Cr̶a̶ ̶

the

Data Science Interview

101+ Data Science Questions & Solutions

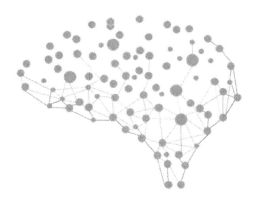

Maverick Lin

ISBN 9781710680133

Foreword ·· **0**
I. What is Data Science? ······························ **1**
  What is Data Science? ································ 1
  Data Science ≠ Machine Learning ····················· 1
  What Makes a Good Data Scientist? ··················· 2
  The Data Science Process Workflow ·················· 2
  Data Science Deliverables ·························· 3
  Writing a Great Data Science Resume ················ 4
  Data Science Interview Topics ······················ 4
  Data Science Interview Process ···················· 5
  Behavioral and Fit Questions ······················ 6
  Data Science Interview Study Plan ·················· 7
  Interview Questions ······························· 8
II. Big Ideas in Data Science ······················ **10**
  Statistical Modeling ······························ 10
  Types of Models ·································· 11
  Occam's Razor ··································· 12
  Curse of Dimensionality ·························· 12
  Interpretability ·································· 12
  No Free Lunch Theorem ··························· 13
  Bias-Variance Tradeoff ···························· 13
  Parallel Processing or Distributed Computing ·········· 13
  Vectorization ···································· 13
  Overfitting ······································ 14
  Regularization ··································· 14
  Observations as Points in Space ···················· 15
  Big Data Hubris ································· 15
  Local Minimas ··································· 15
  Gradient Descent ································· 16
  MLE vs. MAP ···································· 16
  The Cloud and Cloud Computing ···················· 17
  Half-Life of Data ································· 17
  Interview Questions ······························· 18
III. Mathematical Prerequisites ···················· **19**
  Probability ····································· 19
    Overview ···································· 19
    Compound Events & Independence ·············· 19
    Probability Density Functions (PDFs) ············ 20
    Classic Probability Distributions ················ 20
  Statistics ······································· 22
    Central Limit Theorem (CLT) ················· 22
    Law of Large Numbers (LLN) ················· 22
    Sampling ···································· 22
    Sampling Errors ······························ 23

Hypothesis Testing $\cdots\cdots\cdots\cdots\cdots\cdots\cdots\cdots\cdots\cdots\cdots\cdots\cdots$ 23
Correlation $\cdots\cdots\cdots\cdots\cdots\cdots\cdots\cdots\cdots\cdots\cdots\cdots\cdots\cdots$ 24
Linear Algebra $\cdots\cdots\cdots\cdots\cdots\cdots\cdots\cdots\cdots\cdots\cdots\cdots\cdots$ 24
Miscellaneous Topics $\cdots\cdots\cdots\cdots\cdots\cdots\cdots\cdots\cdots\cdots\cdots$ 27
Distance/Similarity Metrics $\cdots\cdots\cdots\cdots\cdots\cdots\cdots\cdots$ 27
A/B Testing $\cdots\cdots\cdots\cdots\cdots\cdots\cdots\cdots\cdots\cdots\cdots\cdots\cdots$ 28
Interview Questions $\cdots\cdots\cdots\cdots\cdots\cdots\cdots\cdots\cdots\cdots\cdots$ 28
IV. **Computer Science Prerequisites** $\cdots\cdots\cdots\cdots\cdots\cdots\cdots$ **30**
Big O Notation $\cdots\cdots\cdots\cdots\cdots\cdots\cdots\cdots\cdots\cdots\cdots\cdots$ 30
Data Structures $\cdots\cdots\cdots\cdots\cdots\cdots\cdots\cdots\cdots\cdots\cdots\cdots$ 30
Algorithms $\cdots\cdots\cdots\cdots\cdots\cdots\cdots\cdots\cdots\cdots\cdots\cdots\cdots$ 31
Databases $\cdots\cdots\cdots\cdots\cdots\cdots\cdots\cdots\cdots\cdots\cdots\cdots\cdots$ 32
Python $\cdots\cdots\cdots\cdots\cdots\cdots\cdots\cdots\cdots\cdots\cdots\cdots\cdots\cdots$ 33
SQL $\cdots\cdots\cdots\cdots\cdots\cdots\cdots\cdots\cdots\cdots\cdots\cdots\cdots\cdots\cdots$ 34
Interview Questions $\cdots\cdots\cdots\cdots\cdots\cdots\cdots\cdots\cdots\cdots\cdots$ 34
V. **Exploratory Data Analysis** $\cdots\cdots\cdots\cdots\cdots\cdots\cdots\cdots\cdots$ **36**
Types of Data $\cdots\cdots\cdots\cdots\cdots\cdots\cdots\cdots\cdots\cdots\cdots\cdots\cdots$ 36
Data Formats $\cdots\cdots\cdots\cdots\cdots\cdots\cdots\cdots\cdots\cdots\cdots\cdots\cdots$ 37
Descriptive Statistics $\cdots\cdots\cdots\cdots\cdots\cdots\cdots\cdots\cdots\cdots$ 38
Data Cleaning $\cdots\cdots\cdots\cdots\cdots\cdots\cdots\cdots\cdots\cdots\cdots\cdots\cdots$ 38
Visualization $\cdots\cdots\cdots\cdots\cdots\cdots\cdots\cdots\cdots\cdots\cdots\cdots\cdots$ 40
Interview Questions $\cdots\cdots\cdots\cdots\cdots\cdots\cdots\cdots\cdots\cdots\cdots$ 40
VI. **Feature Engineering** $\cdots\cdots\cdots\cdots\cdots\cdots\cdots\cdots\cdots\cdots$ **41**
Feature Engineering Quantitative Data $\cdots\cdots\cdots\cdots\cdots$ 41
Feature Engineering Categorical Data $\cdots\cdots\cdots\cdots\cdots$ 42
Feature Engineering Text Data $\cdots\cdots\cdots\cdots\cdots\cdots\cdots\cdots$ 42
Interview Questions $\cdots\cdots\cdots\cdots\cdots\cdots\cdots\cdots\cdots\cdots\cdots$ 43
VII. **Evaluation Metrics** $\cdots\cdots\cdots\cdots\cdots\cdots\cdots\cdots\cdots\cdots$ **44**
Classification $\cdots\cdots\cdots\cdots\cdots\cdots\cdots\cdots\cdots\cdots\cdots\cdots\cdots$ 44
Regression $\cdots\cdots\cdots\cdots\cdots\cdots\cdots\cdots\cdots\cdots\cdots\cdots\cdots$ 44
Evaluation Environment $\cdots\cdots\cdots\cdots\cdots\cdots\cdots\cdots\cdots\cdots$ 45
Interview Questions $\cdots\cdots\cdots\cdots\cdots\cdots\cdots\cdots\cdots\cdots\cdots$ 45
VIII. **Supervised Learning Algorithms** $\cdots\cdots\cdots\cdots\cdots\cdots$ **46**
k-Nearest Neighbors (k-NN) $\cdots\cdots\cdots\cdots\cdots\cdots\cdots\cdots$ 46
Linear Regression $\cdots\cdots\cdots\cdots\cdots\cdots\cdots\cdots\cdots\cdots\cdots\cdots$ 47
Logistic Regression $\cdots\cdots\cdots\cdots\cdots\cdots\cdots\cdots\cdots\cdots\cdots$ 48
Naive Bayes Classifier $\cdots\cdots\cdots\cdots\cdots\cdots\cdots\cdots\cdots\cdots$ 49
Support Vector Machines (SVMs) $\cdots\cdots\cdots\cdots\cdots\cdots\cdots$ 50
Decision Trees $\cdots\cdots\cdots\cdots\cdots\cdots\cdots\cdots\cdots\cdots\cdots\cdots\cdots$ 52
Bagging (Random Forest) $\cdots\cdots\cdots\cdots\cdots\cdots\cdots\cdots\cdots$ 54
Boosting (AdaBoost) $\cdots\cdots\cdots\cdots\cdots\cdots\cdots\cdots\cdots\cdots\cdots$ 55
Neural Networks $\cdots\cdots\cdots\cdots\cdots\cdots\cdots\cdots\cdots\cdots\cdots\cdots$ 56
Interview Questions $\cdots\cdots\cdots\cdots\cdots\cdots\cdots\cdots\cdots\cdots\cdots$ 59
IX. **Unsupervised Learning Algorithms** $\cdots\cdots\cdots\cdots\cdots\cdots$ **60**

k-Means Clustering $\cdots\cdots$ 60
Hierarchical Clustering $\cdots\cdots$ 61
Principal Component Analysis (PCA) $\cdots\cdots$ 62
Autoencoders $\cdots\cdots$ 63
Self-Organizing Maps $\cdots\cdots$ 64
Additional $\cdots\cdots$ 65
Interview Questions $\cdots\cdots$ 65
X. **Reinforcement Learning Algorithms** $\cdots\cdots$ **67**
Markov Decision Processes (MDPs) $\cdots\cdots$ 67
Exploration vs. Exploitation $\cdots\cdots$ 68
Q-Learning $\cdots\cdots$ 69
Deep Q-Learning $\cdots\cdots$ 70
Interview Questions $\cdots\cdots$ 72
XI. **Additional Data Science Tools** $\cdots\cdots$ **73**
Graph Theory $\cdots\cdots$ 73
ARIMA $\cdots\cdots$ 74
Simulation Modeling $\cdots\cdots$ 74
Linear Programming $\cdots\cdots$ 75
XII. **What Data Science Means at...** $\cdots\cdots$ **76**
J.P. Morgan $\cdots\cdots$ 77
XTX Markets $\cdots\cdots$ 77
Citadel LLC $\cdots\cdots$ 77
Amazon $\cdots\cdots$ 77
Facebook $\cdots\cdots$ 77
Spotify $\cdots\cdots$ 77
Kaggle $\cdots\cdots$ 77
DeepMind $\cdots\cdots$ 78
McKinsey & Company $\cdots\cdots$ 78
Boston Consulting Group (BCG) $\cdots\cdots$ 78
Bain & Company $\cdots\cdots$ 78
Uber $\cdots\cdots$ 78
Airbnb $\cdots\cdots$ 79
NBA $\cdots\cdots$ 79
FiveThirtyEight $\cdots\cdots$ 79
Cambridge Analytica Scandal $\cdots\cdots$ 79
XIII. **Additional Questions** $\cdots\cdots$ 80
XIV. **Solutions**
Solutions to What is Data Science? $\cdots\cdots$ 82
Solutions to Big Ideas in Data Science $\cdots\cdots$ 86
Solutions to Mathematical Prerequisites $\cdots\cdots$ 89
Solutions to Computer Science Prerequisites $\cdots\cdots$ 93
Solutions to Exploratory Data Analysis $\cdots\cdots$ 97
Solutions to Feature Engineering $\cdots\cdots$ 99
Solutions to Evaluation Metrics $\cdots\cdots$ 101

Solutions to Supervised Learning $\cdots\cdots\cdots\cdots\cdots\cdots\cdots\cdots$ 103
Solutions to Unsupervised Learning $\cdots\cdots\cdots\cdots\cdots\cdots\cdots$ 106
Solutions to Reinforcement Learning $\cdots\cdots\cdots\cdots\cdots\cdots\cdots$ 110

Foreword

As I was studying for data science interviews during the summer of 2018, I started to compile a cheatsheet of various data science concepts. My goal was to regurgitate the ideas and concepts in the most concise manner as possible, so that in the future, whether it be a day before an interview or 20 years down the road, I would be able to quickly refresh or relearn the necessary concepts.

After publicly releasing my cheatsheet on Github so that others may find it useful (hopefully you did!), I unexpectedly received an overwhelming interest. I came to realize that there was a wide demand for data science material that is both easily digestible and practical.

As a result, I decided to spend some extra time to expand the *Data Science Cheatsheet* into a *Cracking the Coding Interview* style book. The concepts are more fleshed out, but I tried to maintain the condensed nature of the cheatsheet. In addition to adding several new concepts, there are a batch of interview questions after each chapter to help you solidify your understanding. Also feel free to check out the *Cracking the Data Science Interview* Github page that I have set up (for this book) for additional resources!

I take full responsibility for any mistakes that you may find hidden in the book. If you do find any, please do not hesitate to reach out so I can fix them.

Thank you and happy training!

I
What is Data Science?

The ability to take data to be able to understand it, to process it, to extract value from it, to visualize it, to communicate it -that is going to be a hugely important skill in the next decades. -Hal Varian, chief economist at Google and UC Berkeley professor of information sciences, business, and economics

▶ What is Data Science?
Data Science can be defined as the field of deriving insights and value from data by solving problems in a scientific way. In order to derive insights, data science utilizes tools and concepts from several fields: statistics, data engineering, computer science, and machine learning.

As a field, data science was only established recently. But the process of deriving insights and value from data has been around for a while; quants have been deriving trading signals from data for decades, actuaries have been assessing risk from data for insurance and finance companies for decades, economists have been applying econometric methods to data for decades. So why the sudden increase in "data science" activity?

There are a few main factors:
1. Explosion of Data: new technology has allowed us to collect data from billions of devices all over the world, every second of the day, and store it cheaply. We now have several zetabytes of data and now we can start to think about what insights can be uncovered.
2. Technological Advances: computing advances like MapReduce allow us to process vast amounts of data, technological advances like cloud computing provides easy access to vast amounts of computing power on demand, and hardware advances like GPUs make it feasible for certain machine learning algorithms to work faster and more efficiently.
3. Success Stories: there have been many success stories about leveraging data science in various fields, from quantitative investing to election/sports forecasting.

Main Idea: Data science is all about deriving insights from data. These insights are then used to provide *value to a business*- such as by implementing strategies to boost profits or reduce consumption, optimize a marketing plan, or to provide better recommendations to users.

▶ Data Science ≠ Machine Learning
An important point to bring up is that Data Science *is not* Machine Learning,

since the two have become interchangeable recently. Machine learning is based on the idea that algorithms can identify and learn patterns from data and make decisions with minimal human intervention. Machine learning is appropriate for certain data science problems but other tools are more appropriate for others.

Below are two disciplines that can also provide a suite of tools to help solve data science problems:

- **Operations Research** emerged as an interdisciplinary field during World War II and employs problem-solving techniques ranging from mathematical modeling and stochastic processes to mathematical optimization to simulation in order to improve decision-making.
- **Statistics** emerged as a discipline for collecting, analyzing, interpreting and presenting empirical data.

Both these fields have their own suite of problem-solving and data analysis tools that don't require machine learning. A data scientist that can only think in terms of machine learning will probably become a liability to their organization, since only a small portion of your problems will require ML. Being able to clearly identify the problem and solve it with the right tools is a much more important skill.

So, the take away is that instead of focusing entirely on machine learning, it's more important for a data scientist to have a solid foundation in exploratory data analysis, data visualization, probability and statistics, optimization, mathematical modeling and computer science.

▶ **What Makes a Good Data Scientist?**
A good data scientist is someone who can identify the relevant questions, acquire and clean the right data, analyze that data to obtain results, clearly communicate the findings, and last convert the results into solutions. These skills are widely applicable in all industries (another reason why data science is in high demand).

▶ **The Data Science Process Workflow** Suppose you're finally given a data science or machine learning project, what steps should you follow?

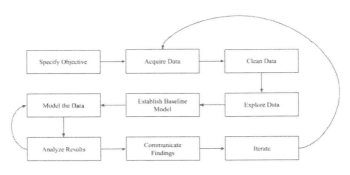

1. **Specify Objective**: what is the business problem we are trying to solve? Are we trying to obtain more customers? Recommend or sell better products? Does the problem require machine learning?
2. **Data Acquisition**: collect the data. What data is relevant? How was the data sampled? Where can we obtain the data? How do we clean the data? Are there privacy issues?
3. **Explore the Data**: are there anomalies? Patterns? How to deal with missing data? How is the data distributed? What does the data represent? What features will be relevant? Can we construct new features?
4. **Establish a Baseline**: create a simple baseline model/score that all future models are compared against. It's no use to have a complex model predict with 75% accuracy when a baseline model already has 80% accuracy. For example, a baseline model for predicting hair color might be just to predict the most popular color.
5. **Model the Data**: build a model, fit the model, and validate the model. What assumptions are we making about the data? Which types of model will perform better?
6. **Analyze Results**: do the results make sense? How do they compare against the baseline model?
7. **Communicate Findings**: Restate the hypothesis, process, findings, and analysis. Ensure results are reproducible. What did we learn? Can we tell a story? What can we do with the findings? What is the business impact of the results? What are the action items?
8. **Iterate**: continue to acquire more data, create new features, and improve the current model.

▶ **Data Science Deliverables**

One of the main questions I had when studying data science was: what does data science actually do? Everything seems pretty cool but what is the end result? I've summarized a few companies and their applications of data science in the Case Studies chapter, but below are a few:

- **Prediction**: predicting if a potential borrower will repay on time or predicting who will win the election next year
- **Forecasts**: forecasting future sales and demand, tomorrow's weather
- **Anomaly Detection**: detecting fraudulent credit card activity or money laundering operations
- **Recognition**: recognizing speech/texts/images
- **Optimization**: minimizing shipping costs, finding the most optimal route or optimal inventory to hold
- **Segmentation**: finding groups of similar customers to customize advertising and marketing or to detect high yield segments
- **Recommendations**: recommending the best products or products to the right customers (think Netflix or Amazon)

▶ **Writing a Great Data Science Resume**

Your resume should concisely summarize your skills and qualifications. Hiring managers and recruiters typically only spend around 6-10 seconds per resume, so really try to put your most impressive items first to make the right impression. Below are a few guidelines:

- **One Pager**: keep your resume simple by limiting it to one page with one column
- **Relevant Coursework**: list courses, education, or certifications relevant to the job (bootcamps, Natural Language Processing, Machine Learning, Statistics, AWS Certified Machine Learning, etc.)
- **Relevant Skills**: list relevant technical skills the job listing mentions (Python, Java, SQL, Spark, Hadoop, etc.)
- **Relevant Projects**: list projects or publications you have completed and links (if possible), but try not to include the common projects everyone has worked on (Titanic, Housing Prediction, Iris Dataset, etc.)
- **Relevant Experience**: list your relevant experience and employment history with impactful bullet points
- **Include Accomplishments**: talk about the specific impact you had; numbers are never bad; business impact (increased speed or revenue by 42%), competition ranking (placed top 5%), etc.
- **Customize**: try to customize your resume to specific jobs (don't send the same resume to every company)

▶ **Data Science Interview Topics**

Data science is a very diverse and large field, consisting of probability and statistics, machine learning, computer science, data engineering, and domain knowledge. As a result, it is hard for someone to be proficient in all areas. Below is a brief outline of the topics that will probably be covered:

- Probability and Statistics
  - Conditional probability (Bayes' Theorem)
  - Probability Distributions
  - Hypothesis Testing (null hypothesis, p-values, confidence intervals)
  - Covariance and correlation
- Computer Science
  - Coding (Python or R)
  - Data Structures (Lists, Hash Tables, Stacks, Queues, Trees, Graphs)
  - Algorithms (searching, sorting, graph traversals)
  - Databases (SQL, NoSQL)
  - Distributed Computing (MapReduce, Spark, Hadoop)
- Machine Learning
  - Supervised Learning (Linear Regression, k-NN, SVM, Random Forest, Gradient Boosting)
  - Unsupervised Learning (k-means, hierarchical clustering)
  - Deep Learning

- General Predictive Modeling (choosing the right evaluation metrics, train and test sets, cross-validation)
- Data Engineering
  - Data Wrangling, Cleaning and Visualization
  - Feature Engineering
- Domain Knowledge
  - Really depends on the company and industry. For example, if you are working as a data scientist in real estate, would be good to have experience in real estate. Or for a NLP role, be prepared for NLP related questions.
  - If you are interviewing for a product-focused company, would be a good idea to know the products along with key success metrics for the company's various products.
- Behavioral and "Fit" Questions
  - These questions are used to determine if you will fit well and get along with the company's culture and people.

The list might be daunting at first, but no one expects you to know everything; it's perfectly fine to say that you don't know something. More often than not, you will have to learn more on the job, so learning to learn is probably the most important skill to have. That, and show that you're hungry, curious, enthusiastic, and willing to learn more.

▶ **Data Science Interview Process**
The interview process usually comprises of a few steps:
1. Coding Challenge
2. HR Screen
3. Technical Screen
4. Take Home Project
5. Onsite
6. Negotiation and Offer

Coding Challenge: this part that tests your ability to code and is probably administered online using Hackerank or CoderByte. The task will be timed and the goal is usually to pass all the test cases that are provided.

HR Screen: this part consists of asking you behavioral questions, "walk me through your resume", understanding your motivation for applying, and asking about your experiences in dealing with certain kinds of situations. You'll also get a chance to ask questions about the role or company, though chances are the interviewer will be not from a technical role, so keep that in mind.

Technical Screen: this will be the more technical part of the process and will consist of questions ranging from computer science to machine learning to statistics.

You should really consider getting *Cracking the Coding Interview* to prep for the coding parts.

Take Home Project: the project will test your coding, analytical, and communication skills and will most likely resemble what you will be doing when you start working. Be aware of the target audience; for example, if your audience is business executives, don't include a lot of technical terms and maybe talk more about potential business strategies.

Onsite: pretty self-explanatory, will probably consist of a series of interviews ranging from technical to behavioral to case studies. Remember that if you made it to this stage, they've already invested a lot of time and resources into you, so they want you to succeed. This is also the point where they determine if you are a good "fit" for the company and the culture.

Offer and Negotiation: Hooray! Probably a good idea to Google a few articles on how to negotiate well at this point. A few different negotiation topics (or levers) include: base salary, signing or relocation bonus, and stock options.

▶ **Behavioral and Fit Questions**
Behavioral questions require you to share examples of specific situations you have been in and how you dealt with them. Some examples include:
- **Teamwork**: talk about a time when you had to work closely with someone whose personality was very different than yours or tell me about a time you handled conflict at work
- **Ability to Adapt**: tell me about a time you were under a lot of pressure and how you dealt with it or what about a time you failed and how you dealt with that
- **Communication**: tell me about a time you successfully persuaded someone at work or a time you had to explain a technical concept to a nontechnical person

The way to approach behavioral questions is using the STAR method:
- **S**ituation: describe the event or situation you were in
- **T**ask: explain the task that you were responsible for in that situation
- **A**ction: explain the steps you took to address the task
- **R**esult: conclude what outcomes your actions achieved

You should make a list of situations or scenarios you have been in *before the interview* so you don't get stuck trying to come up with scenarios on the spot.

▶ Data Science Interview Study Plan

Studying for data science can be quite intimidating- there's just so much to know and the technologies are always evolving. But luckily there's a few main sections you should really focus on (hopefully this book will provide an idea on what to narrow down).

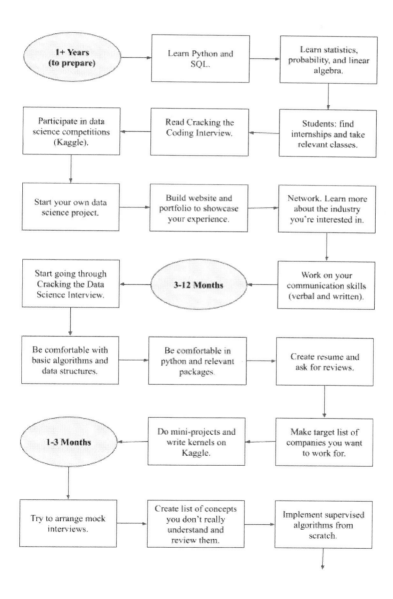

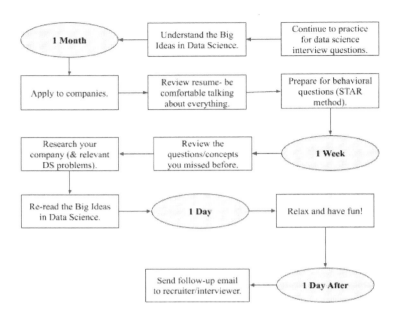

▶ Interview Questions

1.1 Google CRISP-DM. What is it and what are the steps?

1.2 Can you walk me through the steps in a data science project?

1.3 Come up with 5 metrics of success for a:

- Video game with in-game purchases (Fortnite, Minecraft)
- Social networking product (Instagram, Snapchat)
- Advertisement-driven firm•(YouTube, Google)
- Subscription based company (Netflix, Spotify)
- Ride-sharing company (Uber, Lyft)

1.4 What are some key business metrics for a:

- Bank
- Hedge Fund
- e-Commerce site

1.5 How do you test whether a new credit risk scoring model works? What data would you look at?

1.6 What tools and packages do you work with and are comfortable with?

1.7 What is your favorite algorithm? Can you explain it to me in non-technical terms?

1.8 Walk me through one of your data science projects. How did you approach it? What did you learn? What would you do differently now?

1.9 What are you learning about now? How do you keep up with the newest technologies?

1.10 Which data scientists do you admire the most and why?

II
Big Ideas in Data Science

To a man with a hammer everything looks like a nail. -Charlie Munger

Every discipline, whether it be mathematics, physics, or biology, all have several "big ideas" or core principles. This idea is championed by Charlie Munger (Warren Buffet's business partner) who argues that in order to make better decisions in life, it is crucial to understand the big ideas from all disciplines and use them across disciplinary boundaries to solve problems in other disciplines.

Since data science is very much a multi-disciplinary field attempting to solve problems across disciplines, I thought it would be a good idea to compile a list of "big ideas" that data science currently has.

▶ **Statistical Modeling**
Modeling is the process of incorporating information into a tool that can forecast and make predictions. Usually, we are dealing with statistical modeling where we want to analyze relationships between variables. Formally, we want to estimate a function $f(X)$ such that:

$$Y = f(X) + \epsilon$$

where $X = (X_1, X_2, ...X_d)$ represents the input variables, Y represents the output variable, and ϵ represents random error. Every supervised learning problem can be viewed as finding and approximating a function between inputs X and outputs Y.

Statistical learning is the set of approaches for estimating this $f(X)$.

Why Estimate $f(X)$?
Prediction: once we have a good estimate $\hat{f}(X)$, we can use it to make predictions on new data. We treat $\hat{f}$ as a black box, since we only care about the accuracy of the predictions (not necessarily why or how it works).
Inference: we want to understand the relationship between X and Y. We can no longer treat $\hat{f}$ as a black box since we want to understand how Y changes with respect to $X = (X_1, X_2, ...X_d)$ (interpretability).

More About ϵ
The error term ϵ is composed of the reducible and irreducible error, which will prevent us from ever obtaining a perfect $\hat{f}$ estimate.
- **Reducible**: error that can potentially be reduced by using the most appropriate statistical learning technique to estimate f. The goal is to minimize the reducible error.

- **Irreducible**: error that cannot be reduced no matter how well we estimate f. Irreducible error is unknown and unmeasurable and will always be an upper bound for ϵ.

Note: There will always be trade-offs between model flexibility (prediction) and model interpretability (inference). This is just another case of the bias-variance trade-off (covered below). Typically, as flexibility increases, interpretability decreases. Much of statistical learning is finding a way to balance the two.

▶ **Types of Models**
There are many different classes of models. It is important to understand the trade-offs between them and know when it is appropriate to use a certain type of model.

Parametric vs. Nonparametric
- **Parametric**: models that first make an assumption about the shape of $f(X)$ (e.g. we assume the data to be linear) and then we fit the model. This simplifies the problem from estimating $f(X)$ to just estimating a set of parameters. However, if our initial assumption was wrong, this will lead to bad results (e.g. assume data is linear but in reality it's not).
- **Non-Parametric**: models that don't make any assumptions about the shape of $f(X)$, which allows them to fit a wider range of shapes but may lead to overfitting (e.g. k-NN).

Supervised vs. Unsupervised
- **Supervised**: models that fit input variables $X = (x_1, x_2, ...x_n)$ to a known output variables $Y = (y_1, y_2, ...y_n)$. Most problems and interview questions will be based on supervised learning.
- **Unsupervised**: models that take in input variables $X = (x_1, x_2, ...x_n)$ but they do not have an associated output Y to "supervise" the training. The goal is to understand relationships between the variables or observations.

Blackbox vs. Interpretable
- **Blackbox**: models that make decisions, but we do not know what happens under the hood (e.g. deep learning, neural networks)
- **Interpretable**: models that provide insight into *why* they make their decisions (e.g. linear regression, decision trees)

Generative vs. Discriminative
- **Generative**: learns the joint probability distribution $p(x, y)$. For example, if we wanted to distinguish between fraud or not-fraud, we first build a model for what a fraudulent transaction looks like and another one for what a non-fraudulent transaction looks like. Then, we compare a new transaction to our two models to see which is more similar.

- **Discriminative**: learns the conditional probability distribution $p(y|x)$. For example, building upon our fraud analogy, we just try to find a line that separates the two classes (fraud or not-fraud) and don't care about how the data was generated.

▶ **Occam's Razor**

Philosophical principle that the simplest explanation is the best explanation. In modeling, if we are given two models that predict equally well, we should choose the simpler one; choosing the more complex one can often result in overfitting (or just memorizing the training data). Simpler is usually defined as having less parameters or assumptions.

▶ **Curse of Dimensionality**

As the number of features d grows, points become very far apart in Euclidean distance and the entire feature space is needed to find the k nearest neighbours. Eventually, all points become equidistant, which means all points are equally similar, which then means algorithms that use distance measures are pretty much useless. This is not a problem for some high dimensional datasets since the data lies on a low dimensional subspace (such as images of faces or handwritten digits). In other words, the data only sits in a small corner of the feature space (think how trees only grow near the surface of the Earth and not the entire atmosphere).

▶ **Interpretability**

Briefly mentioned earlier, but we'll cover it more in-depth here. Interpretability (in data science) is the extent to which a human can understand the reasoning behind a decision or prediction from a model. If a model predicts a house is worth $300,000 or that a certain e-mail is junk, why did the model do that? A lot of powerful models may have better performance (e.g. being able to predict housing price or spam better), but certain companies or entire industries may not be able to use such models if the results cannot be clearly explained.

An example would be a twist on the trolley problem involving a self-driving car. If a self-driving car had to choose between killing 5 pedestrians or driving itself off the road and killing the driver, what would it choose? And if it did had to choose, what was the reasoning behind the decision? Another important consideration in this problem would be, was the decision manipulated in some way? An interpretable model can be easily debugged to detect any manipulation while a black-box would be much harder to.

Here are a few interpretable models: linear regression, logistic regression, generalized linear models (GLMs), generalized additive models (GAMs), decision trees, decision rules, RuleFit, naive bayes, and k-Nearest Neighbors.

There's also a whole class of models called Model-Agnostic Methods, which we won't cover here. But if you want to learn more, head over to Christoph Molnar's book *Interpretable Machine Learning. A Guide for Making Black Box Models Explainable.*

▶ No Free Lunch Theorem

The No Free Lunch (NFL) Theorem states that every successful machine learning algorithm *must make assumptions*. The implication of this is that no single algorithm will work for every problem and that no single algorithm will be the best for all problems. In other words, there is no "Master Algorithm" that will be the best algorithm for every single problem. The solution is to test multiple models in order to find the one that works best for a particular problem.

▶ Bias-Variance Tradeoff

Bias is the error resulting from incorrect assumptions in the learning algorithm and the model is too simple (e.g. using linear models when the data is non-linear; high bias → missing relevant relations between inputs and outputs *aka* underfitting).

Variance is the error from sensitivity to fluctuations in the training data, or how much the target estimate would differ if different training data was used; this causes the model to capture random noise rather than the signal due to the model being too complex *aka* overfitting (high variance → modeling noise or overfitting).

The trade-off is the conflict in attempting to minimize *both* bias and variance, since models with lower bias will usually have higher variance and vice versa.

▶ Parallel Processing or Distributed Computing

Parallel processing is the process of breaking down a complex problem into simpler tasks that can be simultaneously run independently on different machines. The results are then combined together at the end. Done right, parallelization can dramatically reduce processing time. The most basic example is addition: suppose you want to calculate the following equation: $1 + 1 + 1 + 1$. We also assume that each $+$ takes 1 second. If we compute sequentially, it will take 3 seconds. If done in parallel, it will take 2 seconds. It might not seem like much of a difference, but when your operations require millions or billions of calculations, you can really save a lot of time.

▶ Vectorization

Vectorization is the process of performing operations on a list or vector instead of on scalar values. Suppose you have a list of numbers $[1, 2, 3, 4]$ and you want to add one to each value. You could use a for loop and iterate over the list and add one to every value (which gets slow if you have to loop through millions of observations). The other way to to view it as a matrix operation and can be done in one step (as opposed to n steps). Certain packages have been optimized for vectorization (NumPy) and is the recommended way to perform calculations since the code is more readable and is generally faster than looping. One example of vectorization is updating weights in a neural network during backpropagation (instead of updating each weight individually, we can update all the weights using a matrix operation).

Note: in Python, for loops are slower than for loops in C. NumPy offers vectorized operations on NumPy arrays (which pushes the for loop down to the C level, making the operation much faster than the for loop in Python).

▶ **Overfitting**

Overfitting is a modeling error when the model we trained basically memorizes the data it has seen, which captures noise in the data and not the true underlying function. One analogy to think about it is you have a test tomorrow and your teacher gave you last year's test. Instead of studying the material on the test, you only studied last year's test and memorized all the answers. On the day of the test, you find out that the test is completely different.

Memorizing last year's test is essentially overfitting. You don't actually learn anything about the underlying topics on the test, so when presented with new questions about the topic, you cannot answer them well (also known as failing to generalize). A model that only performs well on the training data is pretty much useless when presented with new information. Some ways to prevent overfitting is cross-validation and regularization.

▶ **Regularization**

A main problem in machine learning is overfitting or when the model does not perform well on new data because it has essentially memorized the training data. This can happen when the model is too complex. Regularization prevents the model from becoming too complex by adding a tuning parameter that shrinks the coefficient estimates. Two popular types of regularizations are:

- **Lasso** (L1): adds the absolute value of the magnitude of coefficients as the penalty term to the loss function $L(y, y')$: min $\left(L(y, y') + \lambda \sum_{j=1}^{p} |\beta_j| \right)$
- **Ridge** (L2): adds the square of the magnitude of coefficients as the penalty term to the loss function: min $\left(L(y, y') + \lambda \sum_{j=1}^{p} \beta_j^2 \right)$

λ represents the tuning parameter; as λ increases, flexibility decreases, which leads to decreased variance but increased bias (again, bias-variance tradeoff). λ is key in determining the sweet spot between under and overfitting. In addition, while Ridge will always produce a model with all the variables, Lasso can force coefficients to be equal to zero (feature selection).

▶ Observations as Points in Space

Many machine learning models take in vectors of numbers as inputs e.g. [42, 21, 42]. Each vector can be represented visually as points in space. Imagine we have a dataset that has two features: "Height" and "Weight". Our dataset might look something like this:

Height	Weight
5.5	150
5.2	120
4.10	100
5.8	180

We can then visualize these points on a 2-dimensional graph as (x, y) pairs. Building off this logic, we can do the same for 3-dimensions: (x, y, z) coordinates. And so on and so forth. However, anything over 3-dimensions we cannot visualize but we can still think of them as points in n-dimensional space.

▶ Big Data Hubris

Big data hubris is the assumption that big data is a substitute for, rather than a supplement to, traditional data collection and analysis. In other words, it's a belief (and overconfidence) that huge amounts of data is the answer to everything and that we can just train machines to solve problems automatically. Data by itself is not a panacea and we cannot ignore traditional analysis.

An infamous example is Google Flu Trends (GFT), which was a service that attempted to predict real-time flu outbreaks by analyzing flu-related Google Search keywords collected in the US. However, GFT performed terribly; between 2011 and 2013, GFT was wrong 100 out of 108 weeks and the service was discontinued in 2013. It was also discovered that GFT's accuracy was not much better than a simple projection using available CDC data; another example of Occam's Razor.

▶ Local Minimas

Suppose we have a function $f(X)$ and we want to find the point that minimizes that function. Local minimas are the best solutions or points in a corresponding neighborhood; in other words, these are pretty good solutions but they are not the best. The global solution is the best solution overall.

The concept of local minimas is related to the concept of convex and non-convex functions; convex functions are guaranteed to have a global minimum or solution, while non-convex functions do not have that guarantee, which results in models obtaining local minimas. The best we can do is run an optimization algorithm (e.g. gradient descent) from different starting points and use the best local minima we find for the solution.

▶ Gradient Descent

Gradient descent is an optimization algorithm to find solutions or minimas that minimize the value of a given function. Suppose you are wandering around some mountains and you want to find the lowest point that exists. You first look around you and figure out which way is downhill and you take a small step. You then do that again and again until you reach a point where every direction is uphill. You have now found a minima, but it might not be the lowest point in the mountains.

Now, you are guaranteed to reach the bottom if there was only one valley (convex function), but you might get stuck in a valley that is sub-optimal if there were multiple valleys scattered throughout the mountains (non-convex function).

Gradient descent is analogous to you looking for the downhill direction; it starts at an arbitrary point and moves in a downward direction (or the negative direction of the gradient). After several iterations, it will eventually converge to the minimum. The learning rate α is simply how large a step we take; too large of a step-size will result in us bouncing around and never reach the bottom.

Stochastic gradient descent (SGD) is a variant of gradient descent and simply performs the gradient step on one or a few data points (as opposed to all the data points), which allows us to jump around and avoid getting stuck in a local minima. It is computationally more efficient and may lead to faster convergence, but results in noisier results.

Mini-batch stochastic gradient descent (mini-batch SGD) randomly chooses batches of data points (between 10 and 10,000) and then performs a gradient step. This helps reduce noise and also helps speed up training.

▶ MLE vs. MAP

Maximum Likelihood Estimation (MLE) is a frequentist method to estimate the parameters of a probability distribution that best fits the observations. So the two main steps are:
1. Make an assumption about the distribution of the observations
2. Find the parameters of the distribution so that the observations you have are as likely as possible. This is done by maximizing the likelihood function:
   - Write down the likelihood function $L(\theta) = \prod_{i=1}^{n} f_X(x_i; \theta)$
   - Take the natural log of $L(\theta)$: $log(L(\theta))$ (turns products into sums → easier to deal with)
   - Take the derivative of the $log(L(\theta))$ and set it equal to 0; solve for θ
   - Check that the estimate found in the last step is truly the maximum by inspecting the second derivative of $log(L(\theta))$ with respect to θ (maximum if second derivative is negative)

Maximum a Posteriori (MAP) is a Bayesian method to estimate the parameters of a probability distribution by maximizing the posterior distribution. This assumes a prior distribution and updates the prior distribution using Bayes' Rule to arrive at θ.

The connection between MLE and MAP is that MAP is just MLE if we use a uniform prior (or we just assume every value of θ is possible). MLE works well when the assumed distribution you are estimating parameters for is correct and you have a large number of observations n, but can be very wrong when your assumed distribution is wrong and n is small (can overfit). MAP works well when your prior is accurate, but can be very wrong if n is small and your prior is wrong.

▶ The Cloud and Cloud Computing
Cloud computing is the delivery of on-demand computing services over the internet with pay-as-you-go pricing. Computing services include servers, storage, computing power, databases, software, analytics and machine learning, and quantum technologies. Utilizing the cloud is cost efficient, flexible, and scalable, allowing you to only pay for what you use and focus on developing and growing your product or organization without having to worry about IT management maintenance (hardware setup, software patching, etc.). For example, if you suddenly need terabytes of storage or hundreds of compute engines, you are just a couple of minutes away from fulfilling those requirements using the cloud.

Companies of all types are using the cloud for various purposes, from big data analytics to web applications to data storage and backup. For example, Netflix spent 7 years migrating everything to the cloud (AWS), which now runs all of Netflix's computing and storage needs, from storing customer information to recommendation engines.

The top cloud providers are Amazon Web Services (AWS), Microsoft Azure, and Google Cloud Platform, IBM Cloud, Salesforce, and Alibaba Cloud.

▶ Half-Life of Data
A half-life is the time it takes for something to lose half of its quantity: the half-life of a drug is the time it takes for the drug to be only half as effective, while the half-life of elements is the time it takes for the atoms to disintegrate. Information or data also has a half-life; the usefulness of information decays over time and being aware of what kind of data you are working with is important in determining how often you should update your data and models.

For example, if you are building a credit card fraud detection model and working with data from 10 years ago, chances are your model will perform poorly well now. Why? Because the data has changed. The game has changed. Fraudsters have found new ways to commit fraud and the data you used to train your model is outdated.

So understanding the half-life of the data you are working with can help keep your models updated and relevant by updating the data at the right intervals.

▶ **Interview Questions**

2.1 Explain what regularization is and why it is useful.

2.2 How do you solve for multicollinearity?

2.3 What is overfitting and why is it a problem in machine learning models? What steps can you take to avoid it?

2.4 Explain the difference between generative and discriminative algorithms.

2.5 Explain the bias-variance tradeoff.

2.6 Is more data always better?

2.7 What are feature vectors?

2.8 How do you know if one algorithm is better than others?

2.9 Explain the difference between supervised and unsupervised machine learning.

2.10 What is the difference between convex and non-convex functions?

2.11 Explain gradient descent. What is the difference between a local and global optimum?

2.12 Suppose you have the following two lists: a = [42, 84, 3528, 1764] and b = [42, 42, 42, 42]. What does the following piece of code do? How can you make it run faster?

```
>>> total = 0
>>> for idx, val in enumerate(a):
>>>     total += a[idx] * b[idx]
>>> return total
```

III
Mathematical Prerequisites

▶ Probability

Overview
Probability provides a mathematical framework for thinking about the uncertainty of future events.

Experiment: procedure that yields one outcome out of a set of possible outcomes and cannot be predicted (e.g. tossing a die twice)

Sample Space S: set of possible outcomes of an experiment (e.g. S = (1, 2), (1, 4), (2, 1), (2, 2), (2, 3), (2, 4), (2, 6), (3, 2), (3, 6), (4, 1), (4, 2), (4, 4), (4, 5), (4, 6), (5, 4), (6, 2), (6, 3), (6, 4), (6, 6))

Event E: subset of outcomes (e.g. tossing two die such that the sum is 3; E = (1,2), (2,1))

Probability of an Outcome s or $P(s)$: number that satisfies 2 properties
1. for each outcome s, $0 \leq P(s) \leq 1$
2. $\sum p(s) = 1$

Probability of Event E: sum of the probabilities of the outcomes of the experiment: $p(E) = \sum_{s \subset E} p(s)$

Random Variable V: a variable whose value is unknown, or a function that maps outcomes of an experiment to their probabilities (e.g. probability of the sum of two die equals 7; $P(V(s) = 7) = \frac{1}{6}$)

Expected Value of Random Variable V: probability weighted average of all its possible values or $E(V) = \sum_{s \subset S} p(s) * V(s)$

Compound Events & Independence
We can use a Venn diagram to visualize two events: A and B. Areas of the two circles represent their relative probability and the overlapping area is the event {A and B}. Events A and B are single events (or a single outcome) and the event {A and B} is a compound event (two or more simple events or outcomes).

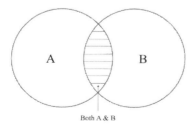

Both A & B

$P(A$ and $B) = P(A) * P(B$ given $A) = P(B) * P(A$ given $B)$. Think about the probability of obtaining both A and B as the probability of first obtaining A, then the probability of B *given* you already obtained A.

P(A or B) = P(A) + P(B) - P(A and B). The probability of A or B occurring is simply the probability of A plus the probability of B minus the intersection (since otherwise it would be double counted).

If events A and B are independent, it means that the occurrence of A provides no information on the occurrence of B. Thus, the P(A and B) = P(A) * P(B) = P(B) * P(A), since the P(B given A) = P(B) (since A provides no information about B).

Conditional Probability
Conditional probability allows us to update a probabilistic model when additional information is presented. Rearranging the formula for P(A and B), we get that P(B given A) = P(A and B) / P(A). This also leads us to the famous Bayes' Theorem: P(B given A) = P(A given B) * P(B) / P(A).

Probability Density Functions (PDFs)

Random Variable X: numerical function that assigns values each outcome of an experiment (e.g. X is the sum of rolling two dice, thus X could be an integer between 2 and 12; P(X = x) = probability that random variable X equals x)
Probability Density Function (PDF): a way to represent random variables; visually it is a graph where the x-axis is the range of values the random variable can be and the y-axis is the probabilities of each value; mathematically is the probability that a random value takes on the value x: $p_X(x) = P(X = x)$
Cumulative Density Function (CDF): another way to represent a random variable; gives the probability that a random variable is less than or equal to x: $F_X(x) = P(X \leq x)$
Quantiles and Percentiles: if the CDF of X is continuous and strictly increasing, then it has an inverse F^{-1}. For each q between 0 and 1, $F^{-1}(q)$ is called the q-quantile of (100 * q)th percentile. The probability that X is below its q-quantile is precisely equal to q. The quantiles work a little differently for discrete distributions.

Note: The PDF and the CDF contain the same information- if you have one you can derive the other.

Classic Probability Distributions
A probability distribution is a statistical function that lists out all the possible values and likelihoods that a random variable X can take within a given range. Probability distributions can be either discrete or continuous (depending on the possible outcomes).

Binomial (Discrete)

Assume X is distributed $Bin(n,p)$. x is the number of "successes" in n independent trials, where each trial is either a success or failure and each success occurs with the same probability p and each failure occurs with probability $q = 1 - p$.

$$P(X = x) = \binom{n}{x}p^x(1 - p)^{n-x} \quad | \quad \mu_X = np \quad | \quad \sigma^2_X = npq$$

Negative Binomial (Discrete)

Assume X is distributed $BN(n,p)$. x is the number of independent trials to obtain k successes, where each trial is either a success or failure and each success occurs with the same probability p and each failure occurs with probability $q = 1 - p$.

$$P(X = x) = \binom{x-1}{k-1}p^k(1 - p)^{x-k} \quad | \quad \mu_X = \frac{k(1-p)}{p} \quad | \quad \sigma^2_X = \frac{k(1-p)}{p^2}$$

Poisson (Discrete)

Assume X is distributed $Pois(\lambda)$. Poisson expresses the probability of a given number of events occurring in a fixed interval of time/space if these events occur independently and with a known constant rate λ.

$$P(X = x) = \frac{e^{-\lambda}\lambda^x}{x!} \quad | \quad \mu_X = \lambda \quad | \quad \sigma^2_X = \lambda$$

Uniform (Continuous)

Assume X is distributed $Unif[a,b]$; X has a constant probability between values $[a, b]$.

$$f(x) = \frac{1}{b-a} \quad | \quad \mu_X = \frac{a+b}{2} \quad | \quad \sigma^2_X = \frac{(b-a)^2}{12}$$

Normal/Gaussian (Continuous)

Assume X in distributed $\mathcal{N}(\mu, \sigma^2)$. It is a bell-shaped and symmetric distribution. Bulk of the values lie close to the mean and no value is too extreme. This gives rise to the 68%-95%-99% rule: 68% of probability mass falls within 1σ of μ, 95% within 2σ, and 99.7% within 3σ. Generalization of the binomial distribution as $n \to \infty$.

$$f(x) = \frac{1}{\sigma\sqrt{2\pi}}e^{-(x-\mu)^2/2\sigma^2} \quad | \quad \mu_X = \mu \quad | \quad \sigma^2_X = \sigma^2$$

Exponential (Continuous)

Assume X is distributed $Exp(\lambda)$. Exponential distribution expresses the probability of the time *between* the events in a Poisson process that occur continuously and independently at a constant average rate λ.

$$f(x) = \lambda e^{-\lambda x} \quad | \quad \mu_X = \frac{1}{\lambda} \quad | \quad \sigma^2_X = \frac{1}{\lambda^2}$$

Power Law (Continuous)

Power law distributions have much longer tails than the normal or Poisson distributions (which typically cluster around a typical value). Power law distributions arise when processes that produce the data involve some complexity, such as feedback loops, networks effects, etc... It is one way to measure the inequality in the world. *e.g.* wealth, word frequency and Pareto Principle (80/20 Rule):

$P(X{=}x) = cx^{-\alpha}$; α is the law's exponent and c is the normalizing constant

▶ Statistics

Statistics provides a mathematical framework to collect, analyze, interpret and present data. The two main branches of statistics are descriptive and inferential statistics. Descriptive statistics are used to describe and summarize the data, while inferential statistics are used to make predictions by taking samples of data from a population and making generalizations about that population.

Central Limit Theorem (CLT)

The CLT states that if we repeatedly take independent random samples of size n from a population (for both normal and nonnormal data) and when n is large, the distribution of the sample means will approach a normal distribution. This allows us to make inferences from a sample about a population, without needing the characteristics of the whole population. Confidence intervals, hypothesis testing, and p-value analysis are all based on the CLT.

Mathematically, we have that: $\frac{\bar{X}-\mu}{\sigma/\sqrt{n}} \to N(0,1)$ as $n \to \infty$, which implies that $\bar{X} \to N(\mu, \sigma^2/n)$ as $n \to \infty$. In other words, as $n \to \infty$, the sample mean gets closer to a normal distribution with mean μ and variance σ^2/n. Note that the CLT is only a statement about the distribution of the sample mean, not the population mean.

Law of Large Numbers (LLN)

The LLN states that if an experiment is repeated independently a large number of times and you take the average of the results, the average should be close to the expected value (or the mathematically proven result). An example of this is tossing a coin 42x vs 42000000x; you will expect the percentage of heads/tails to be closer to 50% for the latter. This implies that large sample sizes are more reflective of reality than small sample sizes.

Mathematically, we have that: $P(\bar{X}_n \to \mu) = 1$ as $n \to \infty$.

Sampling

Sampling is the process of collection and selection of data. The goal is to make a statistical inference about a population from a small set of observations (your sample). Below are a few sampling methods:

- **Random**: every member in your population has an equal chance of being sampled, analogous to putting students' names in a hat and choosing without looking
- **Stratified**: the population is first split into groups and then members are randomly sampled from each group
- **Cluster**: the population is first split into groups or clusters and then some clusters are randomly selected to be in your sample

- **Systematic:** every member in your population is ordered into a list; you then choose a random point and select every kth member

Sampling Errors

Sampling errors are errors introduced to your data via sampling and skews the data in some way. As a result, the samples you obtain are not reflective of the real-world distribution (e.g. only selecting response from Republican voters when trying to build an election model). Even randomized samples will contain some sampling error because they will always be an approximation of the population from which they were drawn from. We can combat sampling error by increasing the sample size and ensuring that the sample accurately represents the entire population.

Hypothesis Testing

Hypothesis testing is a tool used to determine the probability that a given hypothesis is true. For example, a hypothesis might be that population mean is 42 or that the population standard deviation is greater than 42.

Hypothesis testing usually consists of 4 steps:
1. **Formulate the null hypothesis** H_0 and the alternative hypothesis H_A. H_0 is assumed to be true (innocent until proven guilty). *Note*: Rejecting a hypothesis is to conclude that it is false, but accepting one does not mean it is true (only that there is no evidence to reject it).
2. **Choose a test statistic** to assess the null hypothesis.
3. **Calculate the p-value**, or the probability of obtaining the observed results of a test, assuming that the null hypothesis is *true*. Lower p-value $\rightarrow$ evidence against null hypothesis.
4. **Compare the p-value to a significance value** α. If p-value $\leq \alpha$, reject null hypothesis.

So what test statistic do we use in step 2? Well that depends on what hypothesis you are trying to test.

Below are a few main tests:
- **Z-Test:** test to determine if the sample mean is the same as the population mean
- **T-Test (One-Sample):** test to determine if the mean of a normally distributed population is different from a hypothesized value
- **T-Test (Two-Sample):** test to determine if the means of two populations are significantly different from one another
- **Chi-Square Test (Goodness of Fit):** test to determine how the observed data fits some given probability distribution
- **Chi-Square Test (For Independence):** test to determine if two categorical variables are related

Correlation

Correlation describes the relationship between two variables in a context such that one variable affects the other. Correlation is different from act of causing- "correlation does not imply causation". Correlation coefficients $r(X,Y)$ is a statistic that measures the degree that Y is a function of X and vice versa and values range from -1 to +1; +1 means fully correlated, -1 means negatively-correlated, and 0 means no correlation.

<u>Pearson Coefficient</u> measures the degree of the relationship between linearly related variables; $r = \rho_{X,Y} = \frac{Cov(X,Y)}{\sigma(X)\sigma(Y)}$.

<u>Spearman Rank Coefficient</u> is computed on ranks and depicts monotonic relationships; also known as the Pearson Correlation Coefficient between rank variables; $r = \rho_{rg_X,rg_Y} = \frac{Cov(rg_X,rg_Y)}{\sigma_{rg_X}\sigma_{rg_Y}}$, where ρ_{rg_X,rg_Y} denotes the Pearson correlation coefficient applied to rank variables, $Cov(rg_X,rg_Y)$ is the covariance of the rank variables, and $\sigma_{rg_X},\sigma_{rg_Y}$ are the standard deviations of the rank variables.

Note: Correlation does not imply causation!

More descriptive statistics can be found in Chapter V: Exploratory Data Analysis.

► Linear Algebra

Linear Algebra provides a mathematical framework to operate on matrices, which are just rectangular arrays of numbers. In other words, matrices arrange data into rows and columns and linear algebra allows us to manipulate the data in the matrices simultaneously. This helps reduce complicated problems into simpler, more intuitive ones.

Matrices are everywhere in data science, from being the format of training data (where rows are records and columns are attributes) to storing and updating weights of machine learning algorithms to solving linear systems of equations. For example, linear regression can be solved by reducing everything down to a matrix and taking the inverse. So to really understand what's going on behind different algorithms, linear algebra is key.

Scalars, Vectors, Matrices

It is important to make the following distinctions early on:
- **Scalar**: single number e.g. 42
- **Vector**: list of numbers e.g. [4, 2]
- **Matrix**: two-dimensional vector e.g. $\begin{bmatrix} 4 & 2 \\ 2 & 4 \end{bmatrix}$

Matrix Dimensions

The dimension of a matrix is defined by the # of rows n and # of columns m.

$\begin{bmatrix} 4 & 2 \\ 2 & 4 \end{bmatrix}$ has dimensions (2, 2), $\begin{bmatrix} 4 & 2 & 0 \\ 2 & 4 & 0 \end{bmatrix}$ has dimensions (2, 3)

Identity Matrix

The identity matrix, denoted as I, is a square matrix with ones on the diagonal and zeros everywhere else.

$$\begin{bmatrix} 1 & 0 \\ 0 & 1 \end{bmatrix}$$

Matrix Scalar Operation

Involves a scalar (number) and a matrix. The matrix is modified by adding, subtracting, multiplying, or dividing every number in the matrix.

$$\begin{bmatrix} 4 & 2 \\ 2 & 4 \end{bmatrix} + 4 = \begin{bmatrix} 8 & 6 \\ 6 & 8 \end{bmatrix}$$

Matrix Elementwise Operation

Involves two matrices of the same dimensions. The corresponding values in each matrix is paired up, which creates a new matrix. Addition is denoted $C = A + B$, subtraction $C = A - B$.

$$\begin{bmatrix} 4 & 2 \\ 2 & 4 \end{bmatrix} + \begin{bmatrix} 4 & 2 \\ 2 & 4 \end{bmatrix} = \begin{bmatrix} 8 & 4 \\ 4 & 8 \end{bmatrix}$$

Matrix Multiplication

Involves two matrices of size (m, n) and (n, l). In other words, the inner dimensions must be the same. The resulting matrix will have dimensions (m, l). Can be denoted as $C = AB$, $c_{ij} = \sum_{k=1}^{n} a_{ik}b_{kj}$, or

$$\begin{bmatrix} a_{11} & a_{12} \\ a_{21} & a_{22} \end{bmatrix} \begin{bmatrix} b_{11} & b_{12} & b_{13} \\ b_{21} & b_{22} & b_{23} \end{bmatrix} =$$
$$\begin{bmatrix} a_{11}b_{11} + a_{12}b_{21} & a_{11}b_{12} + a_{12}b_{22} & a_{11}b_{13} + a_{12}b_{23} \\ a_{21}b_{11} + a_{22}b_{21} & a_{21}b_{12} + a_{22}b_{22} & a_{21}b_{13} + a_{22}b_{23} \end{bmatrix}$$

If the previous formulas aren't too clear, hopefully the following diagram will help a little:

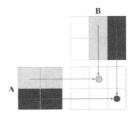

Note that matrix multiplication is not commutative, or $AB \neq BA$, but it is associative, or $A(BC) = (AB)C$.

Matrix Transpose

Involves a matrix and flipping it, denoted as A^T. Can be calculated as $A_{ij}^T = A_{ji}$.

$$\begin{bmatrix} a & b \\ c & d \end{bmatrix}^T = \begin{bmatrix} a & c \\ b & d \end{bmatrix}$$

Matrix Inverse

The inverse of a matrix (denoted A^{-1}) is a matrix such that $A^{-1}A = I = AA^{-1}$. Note that there may not be an inverse at all. The inverse can be found using Gauss-Jordan elimination, Gaussian elimination, or LU decomposition.

Matrix Determinant

The determinant of a square matrix A, $\det(A)$ or $|A|$, is a scalar value. A nonzero determinant tells us that a system of linear equations has a unique solution and that the inverse of a matrix exists.

Matrix Decomposition

Matrix decomposition is the process of turning a matrix into a product of matrices and is done because the decomposed matrices are typically easier and more efficient to solve than the original matrix. There are many different matrix decompositions and each one can be applied to a different class of problems. Two examples are:

- **Lower-Upper (LU) Decomposition**: decomposes a square matrix M into the product of a lower triangular matrix L and upper triangular matrix U such that $M = LU$. In L all the elements above the diagonal are zero and in U all the elements below the diagonal are zero.
- **Singular Value Decomposition (SVD)**: decomposes a rectangular matrix M of size (n, m) into matrices U, D, V with dimensions (n, n), (n, m), (m, m). The final form is: $M = UDV^T$, where D is a diagonal matrix (values only along the diagonal).

Eigenvalues and Eigenvectors

Let A be an (n, n) matrix. A number λ is called an eigenvalue of the matrix A if $Av = \lambda v$ for a nonzero column vector v. The vector v is called the eigenvector of A corresponding to eignevalue λ. For example, let's say we have: $A = \begin{bmatrix} 2 & 0 \\ 0 & 3 \end{bmatrix}$ and

$$\begin{bmatrix} 2 & 0 \\ 0 & 3 \end{bmatrix} \begin{bmatrix} 0 \\ -2 \end{bmatrix} = \begin{bmatrix} 0 \\ -6 \end{bmatrix} = 3 \begin{bmatrix} 0 \\ -2 \end{bmatrix}$$

We have $\begin{bmatrix} 0 \\ -2 \end{bmatrix}$ as an eigenvector of matrix A corresponding to eigenvalue 3. Note there can be more than one pair of eigenvalue and eigenvectors for a particular matrix.

If you think about it, a matrix can be seen as a transformation of another matrix by multiplying or stretching it, compressing it, or flipping it. In short, eigenvectors allow us to understand linear transformations easier since they are the axes or directions along which a linear transformation acts (stretching or flipping) and eigenvalues give you the factor by which the stretching occurs.

▶ Miscellaneous Topics

Distance/Similarity Metrics

Recall that we can view observations as points in space. Such a view provides us with a way to identify similar points by calculating the physical distance between points, where closer distances imply higher similarity. There are several ways of measuring distances between points a and b in d dimensions:

- **Minkowski Distance Metric**: calculates the distance between two points. A larger k places more emphasis on large differences between feature values than smaller values. Selecting the right k can significantly impact the meaningfulness of your distance function. The most popular values are 1 and 2. $d_k(a, b) = \sqrt[k]{\sum_{i=1}^{d} |a_i - b_i|^k}$
  - Manhattan (k=1): city block distance, or the sum of the absolute difference between two points
  - Euclidean (k=2): straight line distance
- **Weighted Minkowski**: also calculates the distance between two points but introduces the idea that in some scenarios, not all features are equal. Can convey this idea using a weight w_i; $d_k(a, b) = \sqrt[k]{\sum_{i=1}^{d} w_i |a_i - b_i|^k}$
- **Cosine Similarity**: $cos(a, b) = \frac{a \cdot b}{|a||b|}$, calculates the similarity between 2 non-zero vectors, where $a \cdot b$ is the dot product (normalized between 0 and 1); higher values imply more similar vectors
- **Kullback-Leibler Divergence**: measures the distance between two probability distributions by measuring the uncertainty gained or uncertainty lost

when replacing distribution A with distribution B;
$KL(A||B) = \sum_{i=i}^{d} a_i log_2 \frac{a_i}{b_i}$

- **Jensen-Shannon**: also measures the distance between two probability distributions; $JS(A,B) = \frac{1}{2}KL(A||M) + \frac{1}{2}KL(M||B)$, where M is the average of A and B. Usually a better choice than Kullback-Leibler Divergence.

A/B Testing

A/B testing is a method of comparing two or more versions of something (app, website, colors, items, etc.) against each other to determine which one performs better. In other words, A/B testing is an experiment where two or more variants of something are shown to users at random at the same time and statistical analysis is applied to determine which variation performs better. "Better" can mean several different things and depends on the objective you are trying to optimize.

For example, a company might want to test different versions of their website layout to see which layout converts more visitors to customers. An advertising company may want to test different versions of the same ad to determine which ad results in more clicks.

The mathematics behind A/B testing is essentially hypothesis testing, where the null hypothesis H_0 and alternative hypothesis H_A might be:

- H_0: the change you made has no effect on the conversion rate
- H_A: the change you made has an effect on the conversion rate

▶ Interview Questions

3.1 Define the Central Limit Theorem (CLT) and its importance.

3.2 Define the Law of Large Numbers and its importance.

3.3 What is the normal distribution? What are some examples of data that follow it?

3.4 How do you check if a distribution is close to normal?

3.5 What is a long-tailed distribution? What are some examples of data that follow it? Why ais it important in machine learning?

3.6 What is Ax=b? And how does one solve it?

3.7 How does one multiply matrices?

3.8 Explain what eigenvalues and eigenvectors are.

3.9 Given two fair dice, what is the probability of getting scores that sum to 4? to 7?

3.10 A jar has 1000 coins. 999 are fair and 1 is double-headed. You pick a coin at random and toss it 10 times and they all come up heads. What is the probability that the next toss is also a head?

3.11 You are offered a contract on a piece of land that is worth $800,000 50% of the time, $300,000 30% of the time and $100,000 20% of the time. The contract allows you to pay X dollars for a land appraisal and then you can decide whether or not to pay $200,000 for the land. How much is the contract worth? And what is X?

3.12 Suppose a life insurance company sells a $240,000 policy with a one year term to a 24 year old woman for $240. The estimated probability that she survives the year is .999562. What is the expected value of this policy for the insurance company?

3.13 Suppose a disease has a 42% death rate. What's the probability that exactly 4 out of 12 randomly selected patients survive?

3.14 A roulette wheel has 38 slots- 18 are red, 18 are black, and 2 are green. You play 42 games and always bet on red. What is the probability that you win all 42 games?

3.15 Walk me through the steps of how you would set up an A/B test.

IV
Computer Science Prerequisites

You will need to know computer science fundamentals, from data structures and algorithms to database management. Basically, everything in *Cracking the Coding Interview*. So go read that and then come back.

▶ Big O Notation

Big O is a way to define the worst case scenario of the running time of an algorithm. In other words, how slow will an algorithm run at its worst as the input size grows? It is essentially a measure of efficiency for an algorithm. It is important to know what the Big O is for an algorithm so we can find ways to improve upon it. The most popular Big O runtimes are (from best to worst; N stands for number of inputs):

- $O(1)$: constant time
- $O(\log N)$: logarithmic time
- $O(N)$: linear time
- $O(N \log(N))$: loglinear time
- $O(N^2)$: quadratic time
- $O(N!)$: factorial time

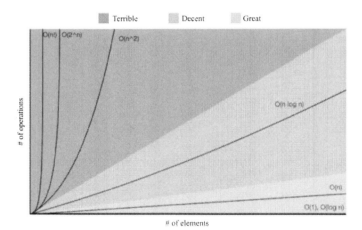

▶ Data Structures

Data structures are a way of storing and manipulating data and each data structure has its own strengths and weaknesses. The appropriate data structures, combined with the right algorithms, allow data scientists and programmers to efficiently solve problems. It is important to know the main types of data structures and the various trade-offs.

Lists: or arrays, ordered sequences of objects, mutable
Tuples: like lists, but immutable
Dictionaries: hash tables, key-value pairs, unsorted
Sets: mutable, unordered sequence of unique elements
Stacks: Last-In-First-Out (LIFO) ordering, so last item added will always be the first one removed (think stack of plates)
Queues: First-In-First-Out (FIFO) ordering, so first item added will always be the first one removed (think queue or line at a movie theatre)
Graphs: comprised of nodes and edges (think social network with people as nodes and edges as friends)
Trees: a special type of graph but has a hierarchical structure, contains one root node that branches out to other nodes
Heap Queue: priority queue, heaps are binary trees for which every parent node has a value greater than or equal to any of its children (max-heap); order is important

	Time Complexity: Average / Worst Case			
Data Structure	Access	Search	Insertion	Deletion
Array	O(1) / O(1)	O(N) / O(N)	O(N) / O(N)	O(N) / O(N)
Hash Table	N/A	O(1) / O(N)	O(1) / O(N)	O(1) / O(N)
Stack	O(N) / O(N)	O(N) / O(N)	O(1) / O(1)	O(1) / O(1)
Queue	O(N) / O(N)	O(N) / O(N)	O(1) / O(1)	O(1) / O(1)

▶ Algorithms

Algorithms are just a set of rules or instructions to accomplish something. That accomplishment could be sorting a list from low to high, finding the shortest path between two locations, or training a machine learning model. Regardless, it is important to understand different types of algorithms so they can be used properly to solve a given problem. Check out *Introduction to Algorithms*. Below we talk about a few essential computer science algorithms.

Searching: goal is to find an element from a data structure
- **Simple Search**: simply search through every element of the data structure before finding the element; O(N) time.
- **Binary Search**: sort the data structure, then find the midpoint. If the midpoint matches your element, great you're done. If your element is greater than midpoint, throw away the bottom half, keep the top half and keep finding the midpoint and tossing halves until you find your element. Similar logic if your element is less than the midpoint. O(log N) time.

Sorting: goal is to sort the elements in a data structure (assume list)
- **Selection Sort**: go through every element to find the smallest (or largest element) and add that to another list. Go through again to find the next element and add that as well. Keep going until you have a sorted list. $O(N^2)$ time.
- **Mergesort**: break the elements down to individual elements then create ordered pairs, which is then merged into groups of four, and so on until final list is created. $O(\log N)$ time.
- **Quicksort**: choose a pivot point and move all elements less than pivot to the left and elements greater than to the right. Then do the same thing again for the sub-lists (left of pivot and right of pivot) until all lists contain one element. $O(N \log N)$ time (average), $O(N^2)$ time (worst).

Graph Traversal: traverse a graph until we find the element we are looking for
- **Breadth-First Search (BFS)**: start at the root node (or random node) and looks at all the neighboring nodes before visiting their children. Utilizes queues to keep track of which nodes to visit.
- **Depth-First Search (DFS)**: start at the root node (or random node) and looks along a single branch all the way to the end before turning back. Utilizes stacks to keep track of which nodes to visit.

▶ **Databases**

Prior to distributed systems, in order to increase the amount of data we could store, the solution was to scale vertically (get more powerful machines) or optimize existing code or queries. Now, we can scale horizontally, or distribute data onto multiple machines. There are a lot of solutions out there and choosing the right database is crucial depending on your needs and application. There is no one database solution that will solve all your problems and in order to choose the right tool, a basic understanding of the trade-offs between potential solutions is important. We now turn to the CAP Theorem, which is the concept that a distributed database system can only have 2 of the following 3:

- **Consistency**: every read receives the most recent write or an error. In other words, all nodes receive the same data at the same time. If a user requests data, he or she will get the most recent data (and not old data). The trade-off is that the nodes need time to update and won't be available as often.
- **Availability**: every request receives a (non-error) response, without the guarantee that it contains the most recent write. In other words, the system is operational (or available) 100% of the time. However, the trade-off is that the data might not be the most recent data (consistency).
- **Partition Tolerance**: the system continues to operate despite an arbitrary number of messages being dropped (or delayed) by the network between nodes. A partition-tolerant system can take any number of network failures that doesn't result in the failure of the entire network. However,

partition tolerance is a necessity; so the trade-off really exists between Consistency and Availability.

Relational Databases

A class of database that stores and provides access to data points that are related to one another and are organized as a set of tables with columns and rows. Each row represents a record (marked with a unique ID) and the columns represent an attribute of the record. These databases usually have strong consistency and high availability (but give up partition tolerance). Examples include: SQL Server, MySQL, PostgresSQL, Oracle Database, and IBM DB2.

Non-Relational Databases (NoSQL Databases)

A class of database other than the tabular relational database. They have more flexible, simpler schemas and include data structures such as document (MongoDB, DocumentDB, Couchbase), key-value (Redis, DynamoDB), and graph (Neo4j). Many NoSQL solutions compromise consistency in favor of availability and instead offer "eventual consistency", or that updates will reach all nodes "eventually" so any reads might not return updated data immediately.

▶ Python

Python now lies at the heart of data science and has emerged as the tool for scientific computing. The solid ecosystem of scientific computing libraries, combined with a simple syntax that allows for easy reading and rapid prototyping has made it one of the most popular tools in data science. Below are some powerful and popular packages:

- **NumPy**: core library for scientific computing, provides high performance for manipulation of array-based data and matrices; provides a wide collection of mathematical functions
- **SciPy**: core library for scientific computing, based on NumPy; contains numerical tools to solve problems in linear algebra, statistics, and calculus
- **Pandas**: core library for data analysis, manipulation, and visualization of high-level data structures; contains many methods for grouping, filtering, and combining data
- **Matplotlib**: creates useful and high-quality data visualizations
- **Statsmodels**: provides classes and functions for the estimation of various statistical models, as well for conducting statistical tests and data exploration
- **Scikit-learn**: based on NumPy and SciPy and provides many standard machine learning algorithms (see Tensorflow and Keras for deep learning)
- **PySpark**: allows us to handle huge datasets efficiently by processing data in a distributed way using a cluster; supports set of higher-level tools such as Spark SQL for SQL and DataFrames, MLib for machine learning, GraphX for graph processing, and Spark Streaming for stream processing
- **IPython**: allows for interactive programming and easy sharing of code

Other great solutions include R (language and environment for statistical computing) and Julia (high-performance language for numerical analysis and scientific computing).

▶ SQL

SQL (Structured Query Language) is the language used to access and manipulate data held in a relational database management system (RDBMS) and is great for handling structured data.

Basic Queries
- return every column and every row: **SELECT** * **FROM** table1;
- return every column and first n rows: **SELECT** * **FROM** table1 **LIMIT** n;
- selecting columns: **SELECT** col1, col3... **FROM** table1;
- horizontal filtering: **SELECT** * **WHERE** col1 = 'expression';
- unique values: **SELECT DISTINCT**(col1) **FROM** table1;
- aggregate data: **SELECT** <u>COUNT</u>(*) **FROM** table1 **WHERE** col1 = 'something'; other aggregate functions are: **SUM()**, **AVG()**, **MIN()**, **MAX()**
- group data by column value with an aggregate function: **SELECT** col1, <u>COUNT</u>(col2) **FROM** table1 **GROUP BY** col1;
- order the results: **SELECT** * **FROM** table1 **ORDER BY** col1 ASC/DESC;
- join multiple SQL tables based on column values: **SELECT** * **FROM** table1 **JOIN** table2 **ON** table1.col1 = table2.col1; (the basic types of joins are inner, left, right, and full)

Data Modification
- update specific data: **UPDATE** table1 **SET** col1 = 1 **WHERE** col2 = 2
- insert values manually: **INSERT INTO** table1 (col1, col3) **VALUES** (val1, val3);
- insert values using query results: **INSERT INTO** table1 (col1, col3) **SELECT** col, col2 FROM table2;

More Advanced Filtering
- **Equality Operators**: = (equal), <> or ! = (not equal to), <, >, <=, >=
- **BETWEEN a AND b**: limits range; values can be numbers, text, or dates
- **LIKE '%expressions%'**: checks if value contains the expression
- **IN (a, b, c)**: check if the value is contained among the given expressions

Frequently Used SQL Data Types
- **Integer (INT)**: stores whole numbers (e.g. 42, -23, 0)
- **Decimal Points (DECIMAL or FLOAT)**: stores decimals or whole numbers with fractional parts (e.g. 4.2, 3.14)
- **Boolean (BOOLEAN)**: binary value (e.g. 0 or 1, True or False)
- **Date and Time (DATETIME or TIMESTAMP)**: stores date and time (e.g. 2000-07-28 1:23:45.678)

- **Text Values (VARCHAR)**: stands for variable length character and holds letters, numbers and special characters (e.g. C3PO)

<u>Miscellaneous</u>
- **Aliases**: can rename columns, tables, subqueries, etc.; **SELECT** col1 **AS** something **FROM** table1;
- **Views**: virtual tables that are created using SQL queries but do not store data; restrict users from directly accessing a table and allow them to access views instead; **CREATE VIEW** v1 **AS SELECT** col1 **FROM** table1 **WHERE**...

▶ **Interview Questions**
4.1 Compare R and Python.

4.2 What libraries for data analysis do you know in Python/R?

4.3 What are constraints in SQL?

4.4 What is a primary key?

4.5 What is a foreign key?

4.6 What is a join? List the different types.

4.7 What is a self-join?

4.8 What is a query? What is a subquery?

4.9 Write a SQL query to get the third highest salary of an employee from table EMPLOYEES with two columns: name and salary.

4.10 Let's say you have two SQL tables: ARTISTS and SONGS. The ARTISTS table has columns artist_name and song_name. The SONGS table has columns song_name and sold_copies. Write a SQL query that shows the TOP 3 artists who sold the most songs in total.

4.11 You have two SQL tables EMPLOYEES and SALARIES. EMPLOYEES has columns employee_name, employee_id, and department_name. SALARIES has columns employee_name, employee_id, and employee_salary. Write a SQL that displays all the departments where the average salary is less than $420.

4.12 Explain the star schema.

4.13 Explain the snowflake schema.

4.14 What is the difference between SQL and NoSQL databases? What are some examples of each?

4.15 What is MapReduce? How would you use MapReduce to count words in a text corpus?

V
Exploratory Data Analysis

Exploratory Data Analysis (EDA) is the initial step to exploring and understanding your data and involves summarizing the main characteristics- numerically and visually. Basic statistical calculations (min, max, standard deviation, confidence intervals) can help provide insights into the data and the distributions. Plots and graphs can be useful in visualizing the distributions and variability, as well as visualizing the relationship between variables.

▶ **Types of Data**
Structured vs. Unstructured
Structured data is nicely organized, which makes it easily searchable. The data is usually stored in a two-dimensional matrix, where rows represent records and columns represent properties of the items (or features). Think of tables as databases or spreadsheets. There is also usually one column that denotes the outcome- the features are then used to predict the outcome (supervised learning).

Unstructured data lacks such structure, such as images, videos, e-mail messages, social media, sensor data, books, etc.. Much of data science is manipulating unstructured data into structured data in order to apply statistical methods and algorithms. It is estimated that 80 percent of data is unstructured and finding ways to derive value from unstructured data is the next challenge.

Quantitative vs. Categorical
Quantitative data are numerical values, such as height and weight:
- **Discrete**: only certain values are possible (gaps between possible values) (e.g. integers)
- **Continuous**: any value within an interval is possible (no gaps)

Categorical data is labeled data that falls into categories, such as hair color or gender, and can be encoded numerically in the following ways:
- **Nominal**: unordered categories (blonde or brown; United States or Canada or China)
- **Ordinal**: order is important (freshman $\rightarrow$ sophomore $\rightarrow$ junior $\rightarrow$ senior; mild $\rightarrow$ moderate $\rightarrow$ severe)
- **Binary**: can take on exactly two values (True or False, Life or Death)

Scalars vs. Vectors
Scalars are simply a single numeric feature (e.g. 42).
Vectors are an ordered list of scalars (e.g. [42, 1, 72]). Can be visualized as a point in space (e.g. [+1, -1] represents the point (+1, -1) in 2D space, [+1, -1, +1] represents the point (+1, -1, +1) in 3D space). The majority of machine

learning algorithms take vectors as inputs.

Streaming vs. Batch

- **Streaming**: data that is being collected continuously and analyzed in real-time (e.g. fraud detection, real-time sport analysis)
- **Batch**: data that has already been collected/stored somewhere and is now being grouped together to perform analysis (e.g. end-of-day transactions, weekly reports, monthly billing)

Big

Data that contains greater *variety* arriving in increasing *volumes* and with ever-higher *velocity* (3 Vs).

Temporal

Data that varies and is collected over time (e.g. rainfall, stock prices).

Geospatial

Data with location information (cell phone calls or texts, credit card purchases, earthquakes).

Dark

Data that is collected and stored by organizations during regular business activities but are not used at all for any other purpose, such as analytics or monetization. Called dark data because like dark matter (which comprises of around 85% of the matter in the universe), dark data makes up most of an organization's data. The main reason that businesses do not analyze their dark data is because of the amount of resources it would take and the difficulty of having that data analyzed.

► **Data Formats**

Some popular data formats are:

- **Comma-Separated Values (CSV)**: text file that uses a comma to separate values and each line of the file is a data record (which consists of one or more fields)
- **JavaScript Object Notation (JSON)**: a collection of key-value pairs that is easy for humans to read and write, and easy for machines to parse and generate; great for exchanging data over the web
- **SQL Database**: SQL (Structured Query Language) allows you to manage and query data held in a relational database management system (RDBMS)

▶ Descriptive Statistics
Descriptive statistics provide a way of capturing properties of a data set.

Centrality Measures- describes the center around which the data is distributed
- **Arithmetic Mean:** $\mu_X = \frac{1}{n}\sum x$. sum of values divided by the number of values (sensitive to outliers)
- **Weighted Mean:** $\mu_X = \frac{1}{n}\frac{\sum w_i x_i}{\sum x_i}$. sum of values times a weight divided by sum of the weights
- **Trimmed Mean:** sum of values after dropping outliers (more robust than arithmetic mean)
- **Geometric Mean:** $\sqrt[n]{a_1...a_n}$. nth root of the product of n values, useful for averaging ratios
- **Median:** middle value among a data set ($\frac{1}{2}$ of data lies below and $\frac{1}{2}$ above) (robust to outliers)
- **Mode:** most frequent element in a data set

Variability Measures- describes how spread out or dispersed the data values are from the center
- **Standard Deviation:** $\sigma = \sqrt{\frac{\sum_{i=1}^{N}(x_i-\bar{x})^2}{N-1}}$. measures the sum of squares differences between the individual elements and the mean
- **Variance:** $V = \sigma^2$. square of the standard deviation
- **Mean Absolute Deviation:** $\frac{1}{n}\sum_{i=1}^{n}|x_i - \mu|$, or the mean of the absolute value of the deviations from the mean μ
- **Range:** difference between largest and smallest value in a dataset

▶ Data Cleaning
Garbage in, garbage out. Quality data beats fancy algorithms.

Data cleaning (or data wrangling) is the process of turning raw, dirty data into a clean and analyzable data set. This is done by detecting and removing incorrect data, replacing or modifying missing data, and reformatting the data so that it is consistent with other data sets. Data scientists actually spend around 80% of their time finding and cleaning data, while the rest of the 20% is on actual data analysis (Pareto's Principle).

High Quality Data Criteria
- **Validity**: degree to which data conforms to defined constraints
  - **Data-Type Constraints**: values in a particular column must be of a particular data type (e.g., boolean, date, numerical, etc.)
  - **Range Constraints**: numbers or dates should fall within a certain range (e.g. no data from year 2042 or -42)
  - **Mandatory Constraints**: certain columns cannot be empty
  - **Unique Constraints**: a field, or a combination of fields, must be

unique across a dataset (e.g. two people cannot have the same social security number)
- **Set-Membership Constraints**: values of a column come from a set of discrete values (e.g. person's eye color may be brown, blue, or green)
- **Regular Expression Patterns**: values must conform to a certain pattern (e.g. phone numbers may be required to have the pattern (xxx)—xxx–xxxx)
- **Cross-Field Validation**: certain conditions that use values from multiple fields must hold (e.g. a patient's date of discharge from a hospital cannot be earlier than the date of admission)
- **Accuracy**: degree to which the data is close to the true values (e.g. data says Joe has blue eyes (which is valid), but he actually has brown eyes)
- **Completeness**: degree to which all required measures are known
- **Consistency**: degree to which a set of measures are equivalent in across systems. Inconsistency arises when two datasets contradict (e.g. Joe has 2 kids in dataset A but 3 kids in dataset B)
- **Uniformity**: degree to which values are specified using the same units of measure in all systems (e.g. metric vs. imperial units, USD vs. GBP)

The Workflow
The process to produce high-quality data:
- **Inspection**: detecting corrupt, incorrect, or inconsistent data
  - **Data Profiling**: compile summary statistics of the data (e.g. number of missing values, unique values, descriptive statistics, etc.)
  - **Visualizations**: graphs can help visualize the distribution of the data and help detect outlier
- **Cleaning**: dealing with erroneous data found during inspection
  - **Irrelevant Data**: drop data not relevant to the problem at hand
  - **Drop Duplicates**: remove duplicates that might have occurred when merging datasets or recorded multiple times by accident
  - **Type Conversion**: make sure data is converted properly (e.g. numbers should be numbers, dates as datetime or Timestamp, categories as numbers, etc.)
  - **Syntax Errors**: remove white spaces and fix typos (e.g. "femAle", "female", → "Female")
  - **Standardize**: reformat data so that they are all the same format (e.g. converting centimeters to meters, Smith, John to John Smith, UNIX to UTC)
  - **Scaling**: transforming the data so that they lie on the same range (e.g. scale ACT AND SAT data between 0 and 100 so they can be compared)
  - **Normalization**: transforming the data so that it can be described as a normal distribution (e.g. useful if the statistical model to be used assumes the data to be normally distributed)

- *Missing Values*: can drop records containing a missing value, impute with a reasonable guess or the mean/median, or use linear regression to predict the missing value. Can also fill in the missing data using similar data points.
- *Outliers*: remove suspicious data that is unlikely to happen, perhaps an error that arose during data collection or processing
- *Cross-Datasets Errors*: reconcile data that contradict each other
- **Verification**: check that after cleaning, the data still conforms to the rules and constraints
- **Report**: generate reports on how healthy or clean the data is, what changes were made, which rules were broken and how many times they were broken

Note: When cleaning data, always maintain both the raw data and the cleaned version(s). The raw data should be kept intact and preserved for future use. Any type of data cleaning/analysis should be done on a copy of the raw data.

▶ **Visualization**
Some commonly used plots for EDA are:
- **Histograms**: to check the distribution of a specific variable
- **Scatter Plots**: to check the dependency between two variables
- **Maps**: to show distribution of a variable on a regional or world map
- **Feature Correlation Plot** (heatmap): to understand the dependencies between multiple variables
- **Time Series Plots**: to identify trends and seasonality in time series

▶ **Interview Questions**
5.1 Explain why data cleaning is so important.

5.2 What is exploratory data analysis and why is it important.

5.3 Suppose you work for a cloud storage company and you analyze the amount of content uploaded every month. During early November, you notice a spike in picture uploads. What could be the cause of the spike and how would you test for it?

5.4 How would you go about to produce high quality data?

5.5 How do you inspect and deal with missing data?

5.6 What is the standard deviation of the following: [4, 2, 7, 12, 17, 6]?

VI
Feature Engineering

Feature engineering is the process of using domain knowledge to create features or input variables that help machine learning algorithms perform better. Performed correctly, it can help increase the predictive power of your models. As Andrew Ng puts it:

Coming up with features is difficult, time-consuming, requires expert knowledge. "Applied machine learning" is basically feature engineering.

The features used to train your models have a huge influence on the performance of the model- some features will be more influential than others on model accuracy, while irrelevant features can increase the complexity of the model and add noise to the data (which can negatively impact model performance). In addition, features may be redundant if they're highly correlated with another feature and can be removed from the data set without any loss of information.

Feature selection methods can be used to identify and remove redundant features that don't contribute to the accuracy of a predictive model. Moreover, variable selection helps in reducing the amount of data that contributes to the curse of dimensionality. Reducing the number of features through feature selection ensures training the model will require minimum memory and computational power, leading to shorter training times and also reducing the common problem of overfitting.

▶ **Feature Engineering Quantitative Data**
<u>Raw Measures</u>: leave data as is (no feature engineering)
<u>Rounding</u>: precision can sometimes be noise, so round data to the nearest integer, decimal, hundredth, etc..
<u>Statistical</u>:

- Box-Cox Transformation: transform data to be more normal; $x_{new} = \frac{x^\lambda - 1}{\lambda}$ if $\lambda \neq 0$. Additionally, $\lambda = 0$ is just log transformation.
- Log Transformation: transform data using the log function to make skewed data less skewed; $x_{new} = log(x)$

<u>Scaling</u>: transform data so that it lies on the same scale

- Min-Max Scaling: scales data between $[0, 1]$; $x_{new} = \frac{x - x_{min}}{x_{max} - x_{min}}$
- z-score Normalization: scales data so mean is 0 and variance is 1; $x_{new} = \frac{x - \bar{x}}{\sqrt{var(x)}}$
- Mean Normalization: scales data between $[-1, +1]$ with $\mu = 0$; $x_{new} = \frac{x - \bar{x}}{max(x) - min(x)}$
- Unit Vector: scales data between $[0, 1]$; $x_{new} = \frac{x}{\|x\|_2}$ and $\|x\|_2 = \sqrt{x_1^2 + ... + x_m^2}$

Imputation: fill in missing values using mean, median, model output, etc..

Removing Outliers: detect and remove outliers visually, using standard deviation (e.g. values $\geq x * standard\ deviation$), percentiles (e.g. values a certain percent from the top of bottom), or capping (e.g. values over x just become x)

Binning: transform numeric features into categorical ones (e.g. values between 1-10 $\rightarrow$ A, 10-20 $\rightarrow$ B, etc.)

Interaction Features: introduce interactions between features (e.g. subtraction, addition, multiplication; features x_1 and x_2 become $x_1 x_2$)

Row Statistics: introduce features that capture the statistics of a data point (e.g. number of NaNs, 0s, and negatives; the max/min/mean/mode, etc.)

Dimensionality Reduction: reduce features by using PCA, clustering, etc.

▶ **Feature Engineering Categorical Data**

Integer Encoding: assign each category to a unique integer (e.g. "cat" $\rightarrow$ 1, "dog" $\rightarrow$ 2, "T-Rex" $\rightarrow$ 3)

One-Hot Encoding: transform data with k categories into numerical vector of length k containing only one 1 and the rest 0s (e.g. we have three categories: cat, dog, T-Rex and we let the first value in the vector represent cat, second dog, and third T-Rex; cat $\rightarrow$ [1, 0, 0] and dog $\rightarrow$ [0, 1, 0], T-Rex $\rightarrow$ [0, 0, 1])

Feature Hashing Scheme: transform features into indices in a m-dimensional vector by applying a hash function to the values (e.g. "quick brown fox" $\rightarrow$ $hash(X)$ $\rightarrow$ [1,3,2,0])

▶ **Feature Engineering Text Data**

Bag-of-Words: text data is converted into counts of the words (e.g. "the dog jumped over the other dog" $\rightarrow$ {"dog": 2, "the": 2, "jumped": 1, "over": 1, "other":1}

Bag-of-n-grams: an n-gram is a continuous set of n items from a text, where items can be phenomes, syllables, letters, or words (e.g. bi-gram example or 2-gram: "the red dog jumped over the other red dog" $\rightarrow$ {"the red": 1, "red dog": 2, "dog jumped": 1, "jumped over": 1, "over the": 1, "the other": 1, "other red": 1})

Term-Frequency-Inverse Document Frequency (td-idf): similar to bag-of-words but instead of taking the raw counts, each raw count is multiplied by the number of documents in the dataset divided by the number of documents the word appears in

Filtering: filtering the text data to remove noise, such as stop words (most common words that don't add value to the sentence) and rare words (not very useful if the model sees "Meeseek" once or twice)

Stemming: clean each word down to its basic linguistic word stem form (e.g. {"playing", "player", "play", "played"} $\rightarrow$ "play")

▶ Interview Questions

6.1 Which is better: good data or good models? And how do you define good?

6.2 Is there a universal good model? Are there any models that are definitely not so good?

6.3 How to deal with unbalanced data classes (for classification)?

6.4 Suppose we are building a fraud detection system and have all the transaction data for the past week for users (date, location, and amount). What kind of new features can we engineer?

6.5 What is TF-IDF?

6.6 What are feature interactions?

6.7 What is an n-gram? What are some possible use cases?

6.8 What is the 2-gram for the following phrase: The answer to the ultimate question of life, the universe and everything is 42. What about the 3-gram?

VII
Evaluation Metrics

Evaluation metrics allow us to estimate errors to determine how well our models are performing.

▶ **Classification**

Confusion Matrix: table that summarizes the performance of a classifier

	Predicted Yes	Predicted No
Actual Yes	True Positives (TP)	False Negatives (FN)
Actual No	False Positives (FP)	True Negatives (TN)

Accuracy: ratio of correct predictions over total predictions; $= \frac{TP+TN}{TP+TN+FN+FP}$

Precision: how often the classifier is correct when it predicts positive; $= \frac{TP}{TP+FP}$

Recall: how often the classifier is correct for all positive instances: $= \frac{TP}{TP+FN}$

F-Score: single measurement to combine precision and recall:
$F = 2 * \frac{precision*recall}{precision + recall}$

Area under ROC (AUC): plots true positive rates and false positive rates for various thresholds, or where the model determines if a data point is positive or negative (e.g. if >0.8, classify as positive). Best possible AUC is 1, while random is 0.5 (main diagonal line).

Log Loss: used to evaluate the predicted *probabilities* (not the final predicted class); $-\frac{1}{N} \sum_{i=1}^{N} \sum_{j=1}^{M} y_{ij} log(p_{ij})$

▶ **Regression**

Errors are defined as the difference (Δ) between a prediction y′ and the actual result y.

Absolute Error: $\Delta = |y\prime - y|$

Squared Error: $\Delta^2 = (y\prime - y)^2$

Mean-Squared Error: $MSE = \frac{1}{n} \sum_{i=1}^{n} (y\prime_i - y_i)^2$

Root Mean-Squared Error: RMSE $= \sqrt{MSE}$

Absolute Error Distribution: plot absolute error distribution: should be symmetric, centered around 0, bell-shaped, and contain rare extreme outliers.

Residual Sum of Squares: $RSS = \sum_{i=1}^{n} (y\prime_i - y_i)^2$

R^2: Measure of fit that represents the proportion of variance explained, or the *variability in Y that can be explained using X*. It takes on a value between 0 and 1. Generally the higher the better. $R^2 = 1 - \frac{RSS}{TSS}$, where Total Sum of Squares $(TSS) = \sum_{i=1}^{n} (y_i - \bar{y})^2$

Adjusted R^2: one downside of R^2 is that it will increase as long as we add a feature; adjusted R^2 is a modified version that adjusts for the number of features in the model, so that an increase only happens if the new feature improves the model more than would be expected by chance; $R^2_{adj} = 1 - \frac{(1-R^2)(N-1)}{N-p-1}$, where N is the number of observations used and p is the number of predictors or features

► **Evaluation Environment**

Now that we know what tools to use to evaluate a model's performance, we need a way to evaluate how good the model really is. The best way to asses a model is to see how well it performs on data it has never seen before (out-of-sample). Below are some key terminology:

- **Training Data**: data used to fit your models or the set used for learning
- **Validation Data**: data used to tune the parameters of a model
- **Test Data**: data used to evaluate how good your model is; ideally your model should never touch this data until final testing/evaluation

Cross Validation will usually be performed to obtain the final evaluation score-this score will (ideally) represent how well a model will perform on out-of-sample data, but it is usually the case that the model will overfit. CV is just a class of methods that estimate test error by holding out a subset of training data from the fitting process. Below are three such methods:

- **Validation Set**: split data into training set and validation set. Train model on training and estimate test error using validation (e.g. 80-20 split → 80% training data, 20% validation data)
- **Leave-One-Out CV (LOOCV)**: split data into training set and validation set, but the validation set consists of 1 observation. Then repeat n - 1 times until all observations have been used as validation. Test error is the average of these n test error estimates.
- **k-Fold CV**: randomly divide data into k groups (folds) of approximately equal size. First fold is used as validation and the rest as training. Then repeat k times and find average of the k estimates.

► **Interview Questions**

7.1 Suppose you have trained many different models. How do you select the best one?

7.2 Suppose you have one model and you want to find the best set of parameters. How do you go about doing that?

7.3 Explain what precision and recall are. How do they relate to the ROC curve?

7.4 Is it better to have too many false positives, or too many false negatives? Explain.

7.5 What is cross-validation? How do you do it right?

7.6 Is it better to design robust or accurate algorithms?

7.7 How do you define/select evaluation metrics?

VIII
Supervised Learning Algorithms

The goal of supervised learning algorithms is to make *predictions from data* by learning a mapping or function between input and output pairs (training data). Formally, the set of input/output pairs is called the training data D and is denoted as: $D = \{(x_1, y_1), , (x_n, y_n)\}$, where x_i is the input vector of the i-th example and y_i is the associated output label. The label can be binary ($+1$ or 0), multi-class ($1, 2... K$, where $K \geq 2$) or real-valued ($\mathbb{R}$).

▶ **k-Nearest Neighbors (k-NN)**
<u>Intuition</u>: assumes that similar inputs have similar outputs; for an input x_0 and a positive integer k, k-NN first identifies k points in the training data most similar to x_0 and outputs the most common label

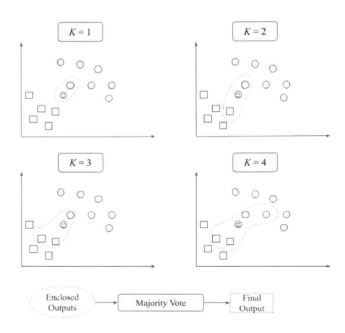

Algorithm
1. Compute distance D from point x_0 to all points
2. Select k closest points
3. Output class with most frequent label in k points

Advantages	Disadvantages
Simple & Interpretable	Susceptible to Curse of Dimensionality
No Training (Lazy Learning)	Slow (as # of training points increase)
Works for Regression/Classification	Sensitive to Outliers/Imbalanced Data
Handles Multiclass Problems	Requires a lot of storage

Improving k-NN

Comparing a query point a in d dimensions against n training examples computes with a runtime of $O(nd)$, which can be computationally expensive $n \to \infty$. Popular choices to speed up k-NN include:

- **k-Dimensional Trees** (KD-trees): partition the feature space and then we can ignore lots of points because their partition is further away than the k closest neighbors; in other words, if the distance to the partition is greater than the distance to the closest neighbor, none of the data points inside that partition can be closer, so they can be ignored
- **Ball-Trees**: similar to KD-trees but use balls (hyper-spheres) instead
- **Grid Indexes**: partition up space into d-dimensional boxes or grids and calculate the nearest neighbors in the same box as the point x_0

▶ **Linear Regression**

Intuition: assumes that the data is drawn from a line and we are trying to find that line by minimizing the distance between the data and our line

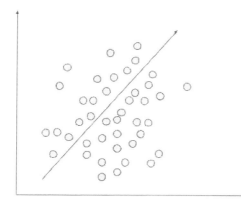

Algorithm: the relationship between input variable $X = (X_1...X_p)$ and output variable Y takes the form:

$$Y \approx \beta_0 + \beta_1 X_1 + ... + \beta_p X_p + \epsilon$$

$\beta_0...\beta_p$ are the unknown coefficients which we are trying to find and ϵ is an error term. The best coefficients will lead us to the best "fit", which can be found by minimizing the *residual sum squares* (RSS), or the sum of the squared differences between the actual ith value and the predicted ith value. RSS $= \sum_{i=1}^{n} e_i^2$, where $e_i = y_i - \hat{y}_i$

How to find best fit?
- **Matrix Form**: We can solve the closed-form equation for coefficient vector w: $w = (X^T X)^{-1} X^T Y$. X represents the input data and Y represents the output data. This method is used for smaller matrices, since inverting a matrix is computationally expensive.
- **Gradient Descent**

Advantages	Disadvantages
Simple & Interpretable	Not great if data is non-linear
Can be regularized to prevent overfitting	Data needs to be scaled

Improving Linear Regression
- **Subset/Feature Selection**: approach involves identifying a subset of the p predictors that we believe to be best related to the response. Then we fit model using the reduced set of variables (Best, Forward, and Backward Subset Selection)
- **Shrinkage/Regularization**
- **Dimension Reduction**: projecting p predictors into a M-dimensional subspace, where M $< p$. This is achieved by computing M different linear combinations of the variables (can use PCA).
- **Miscellaneous**: removing outliers, feature scaling, removing multicollinearity (correlated variables)

Assumptions
- **Representative**: the training data used to fit the model is representative of the population
- **Linearity**: relationship between X and Y is linear
- **Homoscedasticity**: variance of residuals is the same for any value of X
- **Independence**: errors are uncorrelated
- **Normality**: error distribution is normal

Hypothesis Testing: Coefficient Estimates
We can perform hypothesis tests on the coefficients:
- H_0: No relationship between X and Y
- H_a: Some relationship exists

A p-value can be obtained and interpreted as follows: a small p-value indicates that a relationship between the predictor (X) and the response (Y) exists.

▶ **Logistic Regression**
Intuition: assumes that the output is categorical and finds a relationship between features and the probability of certain output

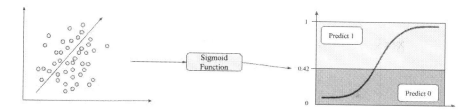

Algorithm: works by predicting the probability that Y belongs to a particular category by first fitting the data to a linear regression model, which is then passed to the sigmoid function ($f(x) = \frac{1}{1+e^{-x}}$), which then outputs a value between 0 and 1 and can be interpreted as the probability. If the probability is above a certain predetermined threshold (P(Yes) > 0.5), then the model will predict Yes.

$$p(X) = \frac{1}{1+e^{-(\beta_0 + \beta_1 X_1 + \ldots + \beta_p X_p)}}$$

How to find best coefficients?

- **Maximum Likelihood**: The coefficients $\beta_0...\beta_p$ are unknown and must be estimated from the training data. We seek estimates for $\beta_0...\beta_p$ such that the predicted probability $\hat{p}(x_i)$ of each observation is a number close to one if its observed in a certain class and close to zero otherwise. This is done by maximizing the likelihood function:

$$l(\beta_0, \beta_1) = \prod_{i:y_i=1} p(x_i) \prod_{i':y_{i'}=1} (1 - p(x_i))$$

- **Gradient Descent/Stochastic Gradient Descent**

Advantages	Disadvantages
Simple	Harder to interpret
Provides probabilities	Not great if data is non-linear
Can generalize to multi-class	Sensitive to imbalanced classes

▶ **Naive Bayes Classifier**
Intuition: assumes with the "naive" assumption of independence between every pair of features and then applies Bayes' Rule to determine the most likely class. Naive because features are usually correlated but this works well in practice.

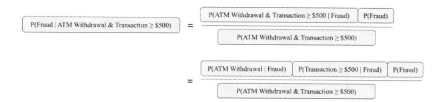

Algorithm: Suppose we need to classify vector $X = (x_1...x_n)$ into m classes, $C_1...C_m$. We need to compute the probability of each possible class given X, so we can assign X the label of the class with highest probability. We can calculate a probability using Bayes' Theorem:

$$P(C_i|X) = \frac{P(X|C_i)P(C_i)}{P(X)}$$

Where:
1. $P(C_i)$: the prior probability of belonging to class i
2. $P(X)$: normalizing constant, or probability of seeing the given input vector over all possible input vectors
3. $P(X|C_i)$: the conditional probability of seeing input vector X given we know the class is C_i

The prediction model will formally look like:

$$C(X) = argmax_{i \in classes(t)} \frac{P(X|C_i)P(C_i)}{P(X)}$$

where $C(X)$ is the prediction returned for input X.

▶ **Support Vector Machines (SVMs)**
Intuition: assumes the output is categorical and finds the *best* separating hyperplane (or the one that maximizes the distance to the closest data points from both classes *aka* hyperplane with maximum margin). Think of the hyperplane as being exactly in the middle- points that fall on one side of the hyperplane are classified as -1 and the other +1.

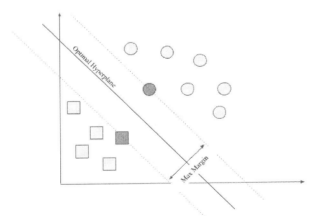

Algorithm: We first define a hyperplane through weights **w** and a bias b (think in 2D: y = ax + b, where a = **w** and b = b). Now we want to find the simplest hyperplane (smallest weights) that separates the points such that all the +1

points are positive and the -1 points are negative. We can now formulate the problem:

$$\min \mathbf{w}^T \mathbf{w}$$
$$\text{s.t. } \forall i \quad y_i(\mathbf{w}^T \mathbf{x}_i + b) \geq 1$$

This is now a quadratic optimization problem and can be solved with any QCQP (Quadratically Constrained Quadratic Program) solver.

Why $y_i(w^T x_i + b) \geq 1$? Because if all the -1 points are negative, -1 times any negative number will be ≥ 1 and if all +1 points are positive, +1 times any positive number will be ≥ 1. Note that *all* points must be on the correct side of the hyperplane- otherwise there is no solution. But what happens if the data is not entirely linearly separable? We relax that constraint.

Relaxing Linear Separability Assumption (Soft Margin SVM)

More often than not, the data is not entirely linearly separable- there will be some overlap between the classes. In this case, we can introduce a slack variable ξ_i that allows data points to be on the wrong side of the hyperplane (for a penalty C, of course). The new problem is as follow:

$$\min \mathbf{w}^T \mathbf{w} + C \sum_{i=1}^{n} \xi_i$$
$$\text{s.t. } \forall i \quad y_i(\mathbf{w}^T \mathbf{x}_i + b) \geq 1 - \xi_i$$
$$\forall i \quad \xi_i \geq 0$$

The greater the regularization term C, the more "strict" the SVM is (allowing few points to be on the wrong side). The lower the C, the more "relaxed" it is, allowing more points to be on the wrong side to obtain a simpler solution. Note that $C = \infty$ is the same as the SVM with a hard margin (first formulation).

Advantages	Disadvantages
Good if data is linearly separable	Expensive to train as $n \to \infty$
Works well in high dimensions	No probability estimates
Kernels can learn non-linear boundaries	Requires feature scaling

Kernels

The kernel trick is a method to use a linear classifier (like SVM) to solve a non-linear problem. Essentially, it transforms the linearly inseparable data into higher dimension, where the data is (hopefully) linearly separable. Popular kernels include:

- Linear: $K(x, z) = x^T z$
- Polynomial: $K(x, z) = (1 + x^T z)^d$
- Radial Basis Function (RBF): $K(x, z) = e^{\frac{-\|x-z\|^2}{\sigma^2}}$
- Exponential: $K(x, z) = e^{\frac{-\|x-z\|}{2\sigma^2}}$

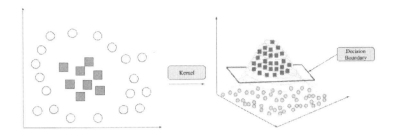

▶ **Decision Trees**

Intuition: similar to k-NN (where we assume that similar data has similar outputs), we build a tree structure to divide the space into regions with similar labels. Each node in the tree contains a simple feature comparison against some value ($x_i \geq 42?$), which results in either a true or false, which then determines if we should proceed along to the left or right child. Ideally, all positive points fall into one child node and all negative points into the other (pure). If not, we continually to split the nodes until all the leaves are pure. To classify an arbitrary point, just traverse the tree and return the most popular label at each leaf.

In other words, the decision tree is asking a bunch of questions that eventually lead to an answer. For example, if you are deciding to wear boots or flip-flops. Is there a chance of snow? No. Is there a chance of rain? No. Is the temperature above 85°? Yes. Wear flip-flops.

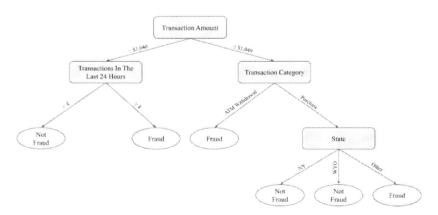

Algorithm

We'll briefly discuss the ID3 algorithm, which is used to build decision trees. First, we define entropy E, which is a measure of how uncertain or impure a set S of examples are, as: $E(S) = \sum_{c \in C} -p(c)\log_2 p(c)$, where C is the set of classes and $p(c)$ is the proportion of the number of elements in class c to the number of elements in set S. When all the elements in the set are the same, $E = 0$ (perfectly classified); when the set is half positive and half negative, $E = 1$ (totally random and equally divided).

Then we can define information gain IG, or how much uncertainty in S was reduced after splitting S on a feature x_i, as: $IG(S, x_i) = E(S) - \sum_{t \in T} p(t)E(t)$, where $E(S)$ is the entropy of the entire set S, T represents the subsets created by splitting set S on feature x_i, $p(t)$ is the proportion of the number of elements in t (subset) to the number of elements in S, and $E(t)$ is the entropy of subset t.

The pesudocode is as follow:
1. Assign all data points to the root of the tree. Set current node to root.
2. Iterate through all features and all splits and calculate the information gain
   - If all points in a subset have the same label, stop splitting the subset and create a leaf node with the most common label y.
3. Select the feature and split that has the highest information gain and set this feature and split to the be the splitting criteria at this node.
4. Continue to recurse on all non-leaf nodes until all points have been labelled or there are no more features to split on. In the latter case, create a leaf node with the most common label y.

Advantages	Disadvantages
Just need to store splits and labels	Prone to overfitting
Interpretable	Instable (not robust to noise)
Works for Regression/Classification	
Handles qualitative/quantitative data	
Indifferent to scale or magnitude	

Other notable algorithms to build decision trees include: C4.5 (successor of ID3), CART (Classification And Regression Tree), Chi-square automatic interaction detection (CHAID), MARS: extends decision trees to handle numerical data better.

Improving Decision Trees
- **Pruning**: decision trees are prone to overfitting, thus pruning is a method that reduces the size of the tree by removing parts of the tree that aren't useful. Two methods to prune are by information gain (removing parts/leaves with lowest information gain) and performance on a validation set (remove parts that result in the smallest increase in error).
- **Early Stopping (Pre-Pruning)**: similar idea to pruning in that we do not want the tree to overfit by growing a smaller tree. In this case, we limit how large the tree can grow by limiting the depth.

Note: rarely do we just use one decision tree. Instead, we aggregate many decision trees using methods like ensembling, bagging, and boosting.

▶ Bagging (Random Forest)

Intuition: since decision trees are prone to overfitting (high variance), we train a large number of decision trees and take the aggregate of the individual outputs (mode for classification and mean for regression). So, for example, instead of just taking the vote of one person, we take the vote of tens of hundreds of people to make the final decision. Random Forest is a bagging (bootstrap aggregating) algorithm and bagging is shown to reduce variance while maintaining bias (another case of the bias-variance tradeoff).

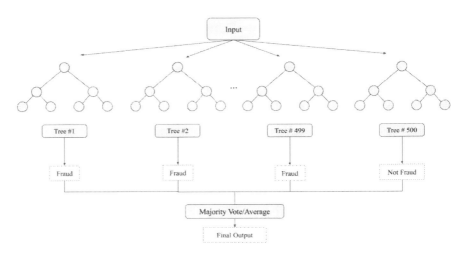

Algorithm
1. First, sample m data sets $D_1...D_m$ from training data D with replacement.
2. For each subset D_i:
   - Train a decision tree- but before every split, only consider k random features, where $k \leq d$ (the total number of features).

The final classifier (or regressor) is the mode (or average) of the outputs from the decision trees.

Advantages	Disadvantages
Reduces variance (vs. decision trees)	Hard to interpret
Can provide feature importance	Not great if features are correlated
Handles qualitative/quantiative data	
Run efficiently on large datasets	
Can handle missing data	
Can be trained in parallel	
Obtain a variance of predictions/scores	
Powerful out-of-the-box solution	
Works for regression & classification	

Improving Random Forest
- **Pruning**: mentioned earlier in Decision Tree
- **Choosing a Good k**: typically a good choice for k is $\approx \sqrt{d}$

▶ Boosting (AdaBoost)

Intuition: the main idea is to combine weak learners into a strong learner. This is done by training models sequentially to focus on what the previous models got wrong by adjusting the weights of the incorrect observations in the training data. This way, it will force the future models to focus on getting those observations correct. The final prediction is a weighted sum of the output from the individual models.

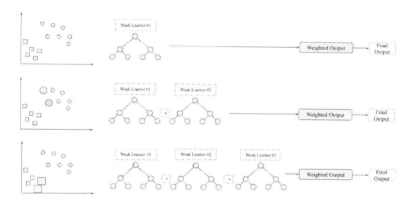

Note: weak learners are defined as any algorithm that does better than random guessing (50%). The implications are quite astounding; by combining many models that do better than a coin flip, we can end up with a strong model.

Algorithm

We'll discuss AdaBoost (Adaptive Boosting) here. Assume we have a training set D with n observations with labels $y_i \in \{+1, -1\}$.

1. We first assign weights $w_{1,1}...w_{n,1}$ for all observations as $\frac{1}{n}$ (all observations are weighted equally).
2. For t in 1... T (where T is the number of weak learners we want to train):
   - Train a weak learner h_t on the weighted sample by minimizing the weighted error ϵ_t: $\epsilon_t = \sum_i^n w_{i,t}$
   - Calculate the optimal stepsize α_t, where $\alpha_t = \frac{1}{2}ln(\frac{1-\epsilon_t}{\epsilon_t})$
   - Update weights $w_{i,t}$ to $w_{i,t+1}$, where $w_{i,t+1} = w_{i,t}e^{-y_i\alpha_t h_t(x_i)}$ for all i
   - Renormalize weights $w_{i,t+1}$ such that $\sum_i w_{i,t+1} = 1$; $w_{i,t+1} = \frac{w_{i,t+1}}{2\sqrt{\epsilon(1-\epsilon)}}$

Advantages	Disadvantages
Reduces bias	Hyperparameters harder to tune
Handles qualitative/quantitative data	Not as easy to interpret
Works for Regression/Classification	Cannot be trained in parallel
Powerful out-of-the-box solution	

The final output is a weighted sum of the weak learners: $y_i = \text{sign}(\sum_{t=1}^{T} \alpha_t h(x_i))$

▶ Neural Networks

Intuition: Let's briefly talk about the brain first. When our brain forms memories or learns a new task, it encodes the information by tuning the connections (or synapses) between neurons (or the basic working unit of the brain that transmit information to other cells). When two neurons interact frequently, they form a bond, which then allows for easier and more accurate transmissions. Thus, the more we practice or rehearse something, the easier it is for our brain to store and recall the necessary information. For example, if we are trying to recognize an animal visually, a certain group of neurons would fire (and others would not), which then results in us concluding, "Oh, a cat!".

Similarly, an artificial neural network (ANN) loosely mimics this model of our brain. Each neuron is just a mathematical function that takes in the output from other neurons as input. When provided with an input, certain neurons in the neural networks will fire, which will then cause other neurons to fire, until we finally get our output. The neurons are arranged in layers and each layer's input is the previous layer's output. The connections (or weights) are trained and tuned by showing the network training data with the appropriate output.

One cool thing about ANNs are that they are universal approximators- no matter what function we are trying to approximate, there is a neural network that can do just that. We can increase the approximation by adding more layers and neurons. But just because we know a network exists, that doesn't mean we can find it.

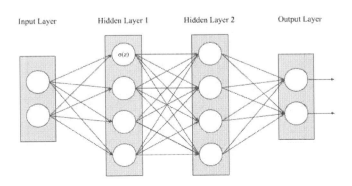

Algorithm

Recall how neural networks require us to train and tune the weights (connections) between neurons so that certain neurons fire for certain inputs by showing the network the correct input and output pairs. The algorithm used to train the weights is called backpropagation, which consists of two parts that are repeated until a stopping criteria is satisfied:

1. **Forward Pass**: the input vector x is fed through the network and each layer's neurons fire and pass along the outputs until we arrive at a predicted output vector

2. **Backwards Propagation**: the predicted output vector is compared with the true output to create an error vector, which is then backpropagated through the network by changing the weights so the predicted output will be closer to the true output the next time around (which minimizes the future error). The learning rate determines how much to change the weights.

The pseudocode is below:
- Initialize network weights $w_0...w_L$ for layers 1... L (usually randomly)
- Set $a_0 = x$ (the input vector)
- While stopping criteria not met:
  - For each layer $l = 1, 2, ...L$
    * Compute $z_l = w_l a_{l-1} + b_l$ (where b_l is the bias term from layer l)
    * Compute $a_l = \sigma_L(z_l)$ (where σ_L is a non-linear activation function for layer l). Return a_L (the prediction)
  - Compute the error vector $\vec{\delta}_L = \frac{\delta_L}{\partial a_L} \odot \sigma'_L(z_L)$
  - For each layer $l = L, L-1, ...1$
    * Update the weights: $w_l = w_l - \alpha \vec{\delta}_l a_{l-1}^T$ ($\alpha \rightarrow$ learning rate, or how much to adjust the weights in the right direction)
    * Update the biases: $b_l = b_l - \alpha \vec{\delta}_l$
    * Update the error vector: $\vec{\delta}_l = \sigma'_{l-1}(z_{l-1}) \odot (w_l^T \delta_l)$ (where σ'_l is the gradient of the activation function σ)

Advantages	Disadvantages
Good to model non-linear data	Not easy to interpret
Great for computer vision and audio	Requires lots of data
Powerful enough to fit any function	Hard to debug
Lots of open-source implementations	Prone to overfitting
Potential for innovation	Alternatives are often simpler/better
	Requires a lot of tuning
	Computationally expensive

Improving Neural Networks
- **Regularization Methods**
  - **Dropout**: involves removing a random selection of neurons from consideration during a gradient step, which forces the network to find new connections and improve generalization

- **Early Stopping**: involves ending the model training early
- **Choosing a Better Activation Function:** recall that each neuron is a mathematical function *aka* activation function. The functions introduce non-linearity to the network and allow the network to learn non-linear functions. Below are a few activation functions:
  - **ReLu** (Rectified Linear Unit): $\sigma(z) = max(z, 0)$. Most widely used because it solves the Vanishing Gradient Problem and allows networks to be much larger.
  - **Sigmoid Function:** $\sigma(z) = \frac{1}{1+e^{-z}}$. Range is between (0, 1) but suffers from the Vanishing Gradient Problem.
  - **Tanh Function:** $\sigma(z) = \frac{1}{1+e^{-2z}} - 1$. Range is between (-1, 1) but also suffers from the Vanishing Gradient Problem.
  - **Linear Function:** $\sigma(z) = z$. Always linear. No matter how many layers you add, the output will always be linear.
- **Normalizing Data:** try normalizing the data between [0,1] to speed up learning (or mean 0 and variance 1)
- **Choosing a Better Network Architecture:** the network architecture is the way the neurons are arranged and connected. Different kinds of networks are suitable for different kinds of problems.
  - **Deep Neural Network (DNN):** contains intermediate layers (or hidden layers) of neurons that represent hidden features and activation functions to represent non-linearity.
  - **Convolutional Neural Network (CNN):** class of NNs that use convolutional, pooling, and dense layers. For example, pooling is reducing a matrix created by an earlier layer to a smaller matrix by taking the maximum or average value across the pooled area. Popular for Computer Vision (CV).
  - **Recurrent Neural Network (RNN):** class of NNs that allow previous outputs to be used as inputs, therefore maintaining a "memory" that stores information that has been processed so far. Long Short-Term Memory (LSTMs) are a fancy version of RNNs and are popular for Natural Langauge Processing (NLP).
  - **General Adversarial Network (GANs):** comprised of two networks that compete against each other; one generates fake examples while the second model has to discriminate (or choose between) the fake and real examples.
  - **Autoencoder:** an unsupervised neural network that is comprised of two networks; an encoder that compresses/encodes the input and a decoder that reconstructs/decodes the compressed input; the main idea is to encode the original data in a more compact way so that the encoded version is almost indistinguishable from the original input.
- **Choosing the Right Learning Rate:** the learning rate affects how much the weights change per gradient step; too large and you might overshoot the minima and never converge; too small and the training will take too

long and might get stuck in a local minima
- **Choosing a Better Optimizer**: the optimzer decides how to change the weights and biases to reduce error during an update step. Popular ones include Adaptive Moment Estimation (Adam), Adaptive Gradient Algorithm (Adagrad), Stochastic Gradient Descent (SGD).

▶ **Interview Questions**

8.1 Describe the regression problem. What is the goal?

8.2 Explain linear regression.

8.3 What is the OLS Regression formula? How do you solve for it?

8.4 Is the intercept term necessary? Why do we need it?

8.5 Compare OLS to Lasso and Ridge.

8.6 What are the assumptions for linear regression? What if some are violated?

8.7 How do you interpret the coefficients? How do you determine the significant features?

8.8 Do you think 50 small decision trees are better than a large one? Why? How would you combine small trees?

8.9 What is the maximal margin classifier?

8.10 What is deep learning?

8.11 How would you build a model to predict credit card fraud?

IX
Unsupervised Learning Algorithms

In unsupervised learning, the model receives the input X but no labeled output Y. What can we possibly do with just X? Well, we can actually learn representations of or detect patterns in the data. The findings can then be used in decision making, predicting future inputs, detect anomalies, etc...

▶ Clustering
Clustering is the problem of grouping data by similarity into *clusters*, which ideally reflect the similarities you are looking for. Of course, we must define what it means for two (or more) data points to be "similar" and "different"; this is usually done using a similarity/distance metric.

▶ k-Means Clustering
Intuition: We assume that there are k clusters or groups in your data and that each data points belongs to only one cluster. Therefore, a data point belongs to a cluster if that cluster's center (or centroid) is the closest cluster to that data point.

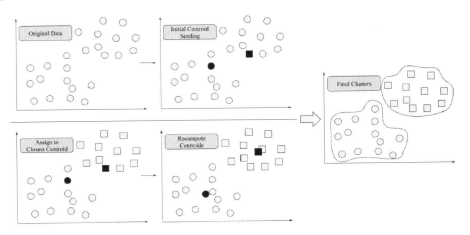

Algorithm
1. Choose a k. Select k distinct random points to serve as initial centroids.
2. Iterate until cluster assignments stop changing (or other stopping condition):
   (a) Assign each observation to the closest cluster centroid (closest defined by the distance metric).
   (b) For each of the k clusters, compute the new cluster centroid, which is the mean vector of all the observations assigned to cluster i.

Note: Since the results of the algorithm depend on the initial random centroid assignments, it is a good idea to repeat the algorithm from different random initializations to obtain the best overall results. We can use Mean-Squared Error (MSE) to determine which cluster assignment is better by taking the difference between all observations in a cluster and the cluster's centroid.

Advantages	Disadvantages
Simple	No optimal set of clusters
Interpretable	Sensitive to scale/outliers
Fast and efficient algorithm	Only handles numerical data
	Assumes there exists clusters to find
	Assumes spherical clusters (not elliptical, etc.)

Improving k-Means Clustering
- Scale or standardize data, remove outliers

► **Hierarchical Clustering**
Intuition: Suppose we don't want to commit to only having k clusters. An alternative is to build a hierarchy of clusters so you can decide the number of clusters later. An added benefit of this approach is that you also obtain a nice visualization (dendrogram) of how clusters are merged (or split) hierarchically; observations that fuse at the bottom are similar, where those at the top are quite different.

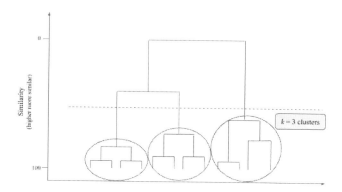

Algorithm (Agglomerative or Bottom-Up)
- Treat each observation as its own cluster, so we begin with n clusters
- Calculate the distance between all pairs of observations/clusters using one of the following linkage methods:
  - Distance between the average distances in each cluster (Average)
  - Maximum distance between two points in each cluster (Max)
  - Minimum distance between two points in each cluster (Min)
  - Distance between the centroids of each cluster (Centroid)

- While number of clusters > 1:
  - Find the two clusters closest to each other and merge them into one
  - Recompute the distances between clusters
- Obtain a dendrogram and determine clusters by cutting the tree at the desired level; each connected component then forms a cluster

Advantages	Disadvantages
Simple	Once two clusters are merged, cannot unmerge
Interpretable	Breaks large clusters
No need to choose k	Computationally expensive
Easy to implement	Assumes there exists clusters to find

Improving Hierarchical Clustering
- Scale or standardize data, remove outliers
- Try the top-down approach (Divisive Method): assign all observations to a single cluster and then split the cluster into two least similar clusters and repeat until there are n clusters (one cluster for every observation)
- Try a different linkage criteria (max, min, average, weighted average, etc.)

▶ **Dimensionality Reduction**
Dimensionality Reduction is the problem of reducing the number of features in your data to reduce storage space, lower computation cost, remove correlated features, and help better visualize the data.

▶ **Principal Component Analysis (PCA)**
Intuition: suppose we have a large dataset and we want to remove some features. PCA allows us to summarize a set of correlated features with a smaller set of independent features that collectively explain most of the data in the original set (or explains most of the variability); the idea of variability is important because higher variance along a dimension (or feature) means that more information is contained, which further implies that the dimension is more important.

Essentially, all we are doing is "dropping" the least important features by creating new, independent features in a lower dimensional space by taking the linear combination of the original features. The downside of such an approach is that the resulting independent variables are now less interpretable.

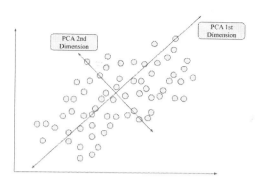

Algorithm

Select a dimension k where $k \leq D$ (D is the dimension of the original dataset)

- Compute the D-dimensional mean vector (or the mean of every feature)
- Compute the covariance matrix of the whole dataset: $\text{Cov}(x) = \frac{1}{N}\sum_{i=1}^{N}(x_i - \bar{x}_i)(x_i - \bar{x}_i)^T$
- Compute eigenvectors ($e_1...e_D$) and eigenvalues ($\lambda_1...\lambda_D$)
- Sort the eigenvectors by decreasing eigenvalues and select the largest k eigenvealues (and the corresponding eigenvectors) and create a D x k dimensional matrix W
- Use W to transform the original dataset into the new lower dimensional space: $y = W^T x$

Advantages	Disadvantages
Removes correlated features	Output is not easily interpretable
May improve algorithm performance	Must standardize data prior PCA
Helps visualize data in lower dimensions	Loses some information
May help to reduce overfitting	
May help reduce noise	

► **Autoencoders**

Intuition: mentioned briefly in the section for Neural Networks, but we'll go a little more in-depth here. While PCAs are by far the most popular method for dimensionality reduction, autoencoders can still be useful. Autoencoders work by compressing the dataset into a lower dimensional space and then recreating the original dataset from the lower dimensional representation. The training is done by comparing the reconstructed output to the original input and minimising a loss function (e.g. MSE). It is comprised of two parts: the encoder (transforms from high dimension to low dimension) and the decoder (transforms from low dimension back into high dimension).

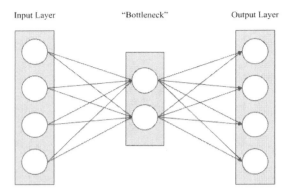

Input Layer   "Bottleneck"   Output Layer

Algorithm
- Initialize neural network and weights
- For 0...X training epochs:
  - Select input X and feed through the network to generate a reconstructed version Z
  - Calculate the loss between X and Z and update weights using gradient descent

Advantages	Disadvantages
Helps reduce dimensions	Uninterpretable
May learn non-linear feature representations	Prone to overfitting
May help reduce noise	Hard to train

► **Self-Organizing Maps**

Intuition: recall how neural networks are comprised of interconnected neurons (nodes). In this case, we also have a network of nodes (arranged in a bi-dimensional lattice) and each node contains a weight vector. We then iterate through the training data and after each observation, we select the node with the most similar weight vector to the observation and update that neuron's weight vector (and its neighbors) to be more like the observation. Over time, certain neurons' weight vectors will recognize certain patterns. The goal is to have the lower dimensional "map" approximate the original, higher-dimensional data.

Why bi-dimensional? The idea is to map higher-dimensional observations into a lower dimension (usually two-dimensions or three-dimensions) so we can visualize and interpret the result.

Algorithm
- Initialize the weights of each neuron randomly
- For 0...X training epochs:
  - Select an observation from the training data

- Find the most similar (or winning) neuron i for the observation using a distance metric
- Adjust the weights w_n of nearby neurons: $w_n = w_n + \alpha h(i)(x - w_n)$, where α is the learning rate and $h(i)$ is the neighborhood function that returns high values for neuron i and its neighbors

▶ Additional

The algorithms mentioned in this chapter are some of the more popular algorithms used. There are other more advanced algorithms such as: Gaussian Mixture Models, Hidden Markov Models, Expectation-Maximization Algorithm, t-SNE, General Bayesian Networks, etc... These are outside the scope of this book... for now.

▶ Interview Questions

9.1 What is the purpose of dimensionality reduction? What is it used for? What methods do you know?

9.2 What is the cluster analysis problem? What clustering methods do you know?

9.3 How do you take millions of Apple users (with hundreds of transactions each and among thousands of products) and group them into meaningful segments?

9.4 Explain what a local optimum is and why it is important in a specific context, such as k-means clustering. What are specific ways of determining if you have a local optimum problem? What can be done to avoid them?

9.5 Is feature scaling important prior to applying k-means clustering? If so, why?

9.6 What is a method for finding an optimal number of cluster in k-means? How do you determine the quality of a clustering?

9.7 What should be the best choice for number of clusters using the elbow method based on the following k-means results:

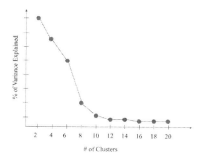

9.8 What are some stopping conditions for k-means?

9.9 Assume you want to cluster 7 observations into 3 clusters using k-means. After the first iteration, clusters C1, C2, C3 have the following observations:

- C1: $(2, 1)$, $(3, 2)$, $(7, 3)$
- C2: $(2, 4)$, $(5, 2)$
- C3: $(3, 3)$, $(7, 7)$

What are the new cluster centroids?

9.10 Explain how you would go about building a recommender system.

9.11 How is k-NN different from k-means clustering?

X
Reinforcement Learning Algorithms

Reinforcement Learning (RL) is the third area of machine learning algorithms and it focuses on finding the best actions in an environment for an agent such that the rewards are maximized; the rewards are emitted by the environment. So, for example, an environment might be a chess game, the agent a player, and the actions are possible chess moves. Perhaps the rewards are maximized when the agent wins the game.

At a high level, RL works by having the agent/algorithm first observe the current state of the environment s_t and then choosing an action a to commit. The environment's state is changed by the action and the environment then emits a numerical reward r that the agent receives. Based on acquired rewards, the agent then updates its policy function (which determines the best action given a state). The cycle repeats until training is complete. This cycle is depicted below:

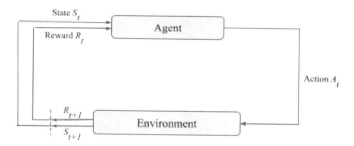

The main challenge is to find the optimal policy function π which defines the behavior of an agent and is defined as: $\pi = P(A_t = a | S_t = s)$. How does it define the behavior? By choosing the best action A_t for any state S_t that maximizes the cumulative reward R, where $R = \sum_{t=0}^{n} \gamma^t r_{t+1}$. In other words, R is the sum of all future rewards, discounted by a factor of γ (a γ of 0 means the agent should focus on short-term rewards, while a γ of 1 means that it should focus on the long-term). One algorithm called Q-learning is one way to determine the optimal policy π in a RL problem and is discussed later.

▶ Markov Decision Processes (MDPs)
MDPs provide a framework for modeling decision making by reducing problems to its essential components, which then helps us more easily formulate a solution. Many problems in RL can be formulated as an MDP, which is just a tuple (S, A, P, R, γ), where:
- S: set of all possible states

- A: set of all possible actions
- $P(s_t, s_{t+1})$: probability that an action a taken in state s_t will lead to state s_{t+1}
- $R(s, s_{t+1})$: reward function where r_t is the reward after going from state s_t to s_{t+1} due to action a
- γ: discount factor between 0 and 1

Let us formulate a MDP for an example RL problem. For example, suppose we are trying to train a RL algorithm to learn the game Pacman. We define the MDP as follow:

- S: set of all possible game states (one state might have Pacman at location (0,0), Blinky at position (0,1), etc... another state might have Pacman at location (2,2), Blinky at (2,3), etc..)
- A: set of all actions for Pacman (Up, Down, Left, Right)
- $P(s_t, s_{t+1})$: probability that an action a taken in state s_t will lead to state s_{t+1} (e.g. moving left in state s_t will lead to state s_{t+1})
- $R(s, s_{t+1})$: reward function where r_t is the reward after going from state s_t to s_{t+1} due to action a (e.g. moving left in state s_t resulted in dying and a reward of -1, or eating a ghost obtained a reward of +1)

▶ **Exploration vs. Exploitation**
Intuition: an intrinsic problem in RL is the exploitation vs. exploration dilemma. The optimal policy for an agent is to always select the best option in a certain scenario or state. For example, if Shoney's is your favorite restaurant and you're hungry, you will always choose Shoney's (exploiting the fact that you love Shoney's).

However, how is an agent supposed to know what the best policy is if it has never encountered it before? Therefore, to learn a policy, the agent must not act rationally by selecting the best option every time, but to venture into the unknown and explore situations it has never encountered before. In our restaurant analogy, this would be you trying a new restaurant (exploring a new restaurant and not exploiting Shoney's).

Thus, there exists a trade-off between performing the actions that lead to the highest expected future reward (exploitation) and trying actions that lead to previously unknown situations in search of new knowledge and hopefully a better policy (exploration).

Algorithm
One way to handle the exploration vs. exploitation dilemma is the ϵ-greedy strategy, where ϵ is a value between 0 and 1. ϵ denotes the probability that the agent picks a random action to explore new situations (exploration). On the other hand, with probability $1 - \epsilon$, the algorithm exploits by selecting the ac-

tion with the highest Q-value, which is just the action that follows the optimal policy π. Wrapping up our restaurant analogy, this would be the same as choosing Shoney's with probability ϵ and trying a new restaurant with probability $1-\epsilon$.

Another version of ϵ-greedy strategy is called the decaying ϵ-greedy. The main idea is to first explore a lot in the beginning of the training session by making all random moves (e.g. $\epsilon = 1$). As time goes on, ϵ decreases by a constant rate α (ϵ decay rate). Near the end of the training session, the agent settles on a lower fixed exploration rate.

▶ **Q-Learning**

<u>Intuition</u>: as mentioned earlier, one technique to find the optimal policy is Q-Learning. The optimal policy π determines the best action for every possible state that maximizes the cumulative reward.

Let's first recursively define a Q-function that follows the optimal policy π as $Q^{\pi}(s_t, a_t) = R(s_t, a_t) + \gamma \max_{a'} Q(s', a')$. In other words, $Q(s_t, a_t)$ represents the quality of an action a_t taken in a state s_t, where quality is the current reward plus the discounted quality of the next state s'. Therefore, for every action in a state, there exists a Q-value; but more importantly, there exists an action with the highest Q-value. The highest quality action defines the optimal policy π, since the agent will want to choose the action with the highest Q-value. Thus, $\pi(s_t) = \text{argmax } Q(s_t, a_t)$.

This may be a bit confusing, so hopefully thinking about a Q-table will help. Q-values can be stored as a 2-dimensional table with all the possible states as rows and all possible actions as columns. Thus, if there existed m possible states and n possible actions, we would have a m x n table with mn Q-values. During training, as the agent chooses actions and receive rewards, the Q-table gets updated. So by the end of training, the Q-table will ideally have low Q-values for action-state pairs that result in negative rewards and high Q-values for action-state pairs that result in positive rewards. The optimal policy is just finding the current state the agent is in and choosing the action with the highest Q-value.

Actions

	a_0	a_1	a_2	...
s_0	$Q(s_0, a_0)$	$Q(s_0, a_1)$	$Q(s_0, a_2)$	...
s_1	$Q(s_1, a_0)$	$Q(s_1, a_1)$	$Q(s_1, a_2)$	...
s_2	$Q(s_2, a_0)$	$Q(s_2, a_1)$	$Q(s_2, a_2)$	...
...	...	...	...	...

(States, on the left, labels the rows)

The last part is how to update the Q-values in the table during training and we use the following equation (α is the learning rate or how much to update the Q-values):

$$Q_{t+1}(s_t, a_t) = (1 - \alpha)Q_t(s_t, a_t) + \alpha(r_{t+1} + \gamma max_a Q_t(s_{t+1}, a))$$

In the early stages of learning, Q-values might be completely wrong, but they become more accurate with every iteration and it has been proven that the Q-function will eventually converge to the true Q-values, as long as all the action-values are represented and all actions are repeatedly sampled in all states.

Algorithm
- Initialize the Q-table with the proper states and actions
- Initialize Q-values randomly
- While training
  - Observe current state s and choose action a from policy (e.g. ϵ-greedy)
  - Commit to action a and observe reward r and next state s'
  - Update Q-values
  - Update current state s to s'

▶ **Deep Q-Learning**
Intuition: one problem with storing Q-values in a 2-dimensional table is that the table might get too large. In other words, there might be too many states (or even infinite states) to store efficiently. Another problem with such a large state space is that the Q-values might take forever to converge and that some states will be rarely visited, so the Q-values for those states would be terrible. What do we do then?

One solution is to use a neural network to approximate the Q-values. Remember that the Q-function is just a function that maps states and actions to a value-thus, we can just replace that function with a neural network that takes a state as an input and outputs a Q-value for every possible action. Since Q-values can be any real values, the task is now regression and can be optimized using MSE. The model is depicted below:

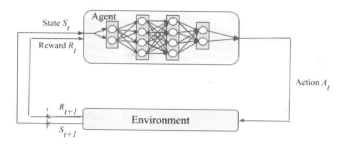

Algorithm
1. Do a feedforward pass for the current state s_t to get predicted Q-values for all actions
2. Do a feedforward pass for the next state s_{t+1} and calculate the max over all network outputs
3. Set Q-value target for action a to $R(s_t, a_t) + \alpha\max_a Q(s_{t+1}, a_{t+1})$. For all the other actions, set the Q-value targets to the same as originally returned
4. Update the weights using backpropagation

Improving on Q-Learning
- **Choosing the Right Rewards**: defining the reward function is crucial in guiding an agent to learn the right strategies. For example, in the Deepmind paper for Playing Atari, they implemented reward clipping, where they fixed all positive rewards to +1, all negative rewards to -1, and leaving 0 rewards unchanged. One downside to this approach is that a normalized rewards system would affect the performance of the agent, since it cannot differentiate between rewards of different magnitudes.
- **Experience Replay**: if you are using a neural network and non-linear activation functions to approximate the Q-value, it might have a hard time converging. One trick is to store all the experiences as a tuple (s_t, a_t, r_t, s_{t+1}); think of it as a memory bank that stores exactly what happened: the current state, the action that the agent took, the reward from that action, and what state the agent ended up in.
  - Then, while training the network, mini-batches from the replay memory bank are sampled and used to train the network. This helps decorrelate the samples by breaking the similarity of sequential training samples (which might drive the network into a local minima) and also prevents the network from "forgetting" what it was like to be in a state it hasn't seen in a while.
  - Think about it as if you wrote down lessons you learned everyday on an index card and then you showed yourself 5 random index cards everyday so you don't forget those lessons.
- **Fixed Q-Target Network**: recall that the Deep Q-Learning algorithm uses one neural network that is used to predict/approximate the Q-values

for *both* the current state and the next state. However, since every time the network is updated for the current state, the approximation for the next state also changes. This oscillation and tail-chasing makes it harder for the network to converge.

- Instead, we can use 2 different networks- one to predict the current state Q-value and another for the next state. Then, every x training iterations, the network to predict the current state is cloned and becomes the network that also approximates the next state. This way, there is a fixed target that occasionally moves and helps the network converge.

► **Interview Questions**

10.1 What are some real-life potential use cases for reinforcement learning agents?

10.2 Check out OpenAI and build a RL algorithm in Python for the game Cartpole.

XI
Additional Data Science Tools

Recall that data science $\neq$ machine learning. Below is an introductory list of potential tools and non-ML algorithms to help you solve a multitude of problems.

Graph Theory

Graph theory is the study of graphs, which are structures used to model relationships between objects. For example, we can model friendships, computers, social networks, and transportation systems all as graphs. These graphs can then be analyzed to uncover hidden patterns or connections that were previously unidentifiable or calculate statistical properties of the networks and predict how the networks will evolve over time.

Formally, a graph $G = (V, E)$ consists of a set V of vertices (nodes) and a set E of edges (connects two nodes together). An edge represents a relationship between the nodes it connects (friendship between 2 people, connection between 2 computers, etc.). A directed graph is where the edges have a direction or order (otherwise undirected).

A weighted graph is a graph where the edges show the intensity of the relationships using weights:

- **Binary Weight**: 0 or 1 weight, tells us if a link exists between 2 nodes
- **Numeric Weight**: expresses how strong the connection is between a node and other nodes
- **Normalized Weight**: variant of numeric weight where all the outgoing edges of a node sum to 1

A graph can be represented:

- **Graphically**: a picture that displays all the nodes, edges, and weights
- **Mathematically**: an adjacency matrix A of size (n, n) (n nodes) and $a_{i,j} = 1$ if a link exists between nodes i and j, 0 otherwise. A weight matrix W expresses the edge weights between nodes of a network. An adjacency list is an abstract representation of the adjacency matrix, and provides a list of all the connections present in the network (weight list is similar).

Applications of graph theory include:

- **Route Optimization**: model the transportation of a commodity from one place to another and the goal is to maximize the amount transported while minimizing the cost of transportation
- **Job Scheduling**: model and find the optimal scheduling of jobs or tasks
- **Fraud Detection**: model fraud transactions and uncover rings of fraudsters working together

- **Sociology and Economics**: model groups of people to see how they will act and evolve over time
- **Epidemiology**: model how a disease will spread through a network and how fast it will spread
- **Chemistry**: model chemical compounds

Python's NetworkX and Spark's GraphX offer graph capabilities.

ARIMA

ARIMA (or AutoRegressive Integrated Moving Average) is used to model time series data (or a sequence of observations taken over time). ARIMA has 3 components:

- **AR (AutoRegressive)** (p): each observation is modeled as a weighted average of past observations plus a white noise "error". In other words, we are using regression where the features are its own past values. p refers to the number of past observations used as features.
- **I (Integrated)** (d): the entire series is differenced in order to make the time series stationary (statistical properties such mean, variance, autocorrelation are all constant). d refers to the number of times the series is differenced.
- **MA (Moving Average)** (q): each observation is modeled as a weighted average of past errors. q refers to the number of lagged forecast errors in the prediction equation.

ARIMA models are usually denoted as ARIMA(p, d, q) and the mathematical formulation is: $y_t = \mu + \phi_1 y_{t-1} + ... + \phi_p y_{t-p} - \theta_1 e_{t-1} - ... - \theta_q e_{t-q}$. Python's statsmodel package offers ARIMA fitting capabilities.

Simulation Modeling

Simulation deals with using computers to imitate real-world systems/processes to understand how they behave over time. We need to make reasonably accurate assumptions about how the system operates (such as the distribution of events), which then leads to the creation of a probability model.

These simulation studies utilize random numbers to simulate possible occurrences for a system over a large number of days and uses statistics to estimate answers to questions. Simulation is often used to help decision making under uncertainty and has applications in numerical computation, algorithms, risk-analysis, and what-if analysis.

For example, the return of complex derivatives whose return is given by a function $f(X_1, ..., X_n)$ of the underlying (random) asset prices $(X_1, ..., X_n)$. If f is linear, then the expected value can be calculated using the linearity of expectation, but it gets more complex if f is non-linear since there is no closed-form solution. In this case, we can simulate the prices of the asset to arrive at the solution. In other words, simulation can be extremely helpful if there is no closed-form solution to the problem we are trying to solve.

Simulation is used in AI for games (reinforcment learning), finance for evaluating derivatives and risk, weather forecasting, computational biology, etc...

Linear Programming

Linear programming is an optimization method for a system of linear constraints and a linear objective function. An objective function defines the quantity to be optimized and the goal of linear programming is to find the values of the variables that maximize or minimize the objective function while adhering to the constraints. The applications of linear programming are endless:

- **Manufacturing**: calculate how to allocate resources (how much raw materials, machines, or labor is needed) to minimize cost/time and maximize revenue
- **Business Operations**: decide what products to sell and how much to sell in order to maximize profit
- **Transportation Optimization**: decide how to schedule resources in order to minimize time and cost; for example, bus and train routes scheduling must factor in travel times, number of passengers, and capacity; airlines must optimize their profits depending on demand, fuel prices, pilot schedules, routes, ticket prices, etc.

Most linear programming problems can be formulated as the following:

$$\text{minimize (or maximize): } c^T x$$
$$\text{subject to: } Ax \le b$$

where c is coefficient vector of the objective function, x is the variable vector that needs to be solved, A is the coefficient matrix for the coefficients, and b is a vector containing the maximum values for the constraints.

Python's NumPy, SymPy, CVXPY, and PuLP offer linear programming capabilities.

XII
What Data Science Means at...

▶ **Finance**

J.P. Morgan

J.P. Morgan is a multinational bank with roughly $2.7 trillion in assets. In May 2017, J.P Morgan released a guide titled *Big Data and AI Strategies: Machine Learning and Alternative Data Approach to Investing*. The goal was to provide a framework for machine learning and big data investing. This includes an overview of types of alternative data and ML methods to analyze them. Below are a few main points:

1. Given the amount of data that is available today, a skilled quantitative investor can theoretically have near real-time macro or company specific data by analyzing relevant market data in real time (and not waiting for monthly or quarterly data to be released). For example, estimating inflation data by using prices of millions of items online or using satellite imaging to assess the activity of oil rigs.

2. The massive amount of data generated needs to be properly extracted, cleaned, and stored before any analysis can be made or incorporated into a trading strategy.

3. Employing data scientists who lack specific financial expertise or financial intuition may not lead to the desired investment results or lead to culture clashes.

4. As more alternative data sets are adopted, old or traditional datasets (quarterly corporate earnings, low frequency macroeconomic data, etc) will lose predictive power.

5. Machines are already dominating short term trading and are becoming more relevant in the medium term horizon, but they will have a harder time predicting market turning points and forecasts that require interpreting human responses, such as those related to politicians or central bankers.

6. Analysts, portfolio managers, traders, and CIOs will eventually have to become familiar with Big Data and Machine Learning approaches to investing.

XTX Markets

XTX Markets was founded in 2015 and is an quantitative-driven electronic market maker (EMM). EMMs profit by buying and selling financial securities and deploying strategies designed to harvest bid-ask spread revenues. XTX has climbed the ranks in currency trading with only mathematical models (no human traders) trained on huge data sets and handles over $150 billion in trades everyday.

In 2019, XTX ran a forecasting challenge to attract potential data scientists to hire with a total prize pool of $100,000.

Citadel LLC

Citadel LLC is an American global financial institution and operates two primary businesses: Citadel, one of the world's largest alternative asset managers with more than $32 billion in assets under management; and Citadel Securities, one of the leading market makers in the world. Data science is applied in three areas: quantitative research, software engineering, and trading.

- **Quantitative Researchers**: glean insights from datasets to help make investment decisions; the objective is to create proprietary algorithms.
- **Software Engineering**: develop tools and technology to bring the trading strategies to the market
- **Trading**: manage risk, identify investment opportunities, and make critical trading decisions in a fast-paced environment

Citadel holds datathon competitions throughout the year at a series of top universities to attract talent.

▶ Technology

Amazon

Amazon is multinational company focused on e-commerce, cloud computing, digital streaming, and artificial intelligence. Data science is prevalent in almost all areas of Amazon's business, ranging from supply chain optimization to fraud and fake reviews detection. Additional areas are: advertising optimization, inventory and sales forecasting, recommendation engines, and optimal pricing structures.

Facebook

Facebook is a social networking website that has more than 2 billion monthly active users. Data scientists at Facebook conduct large-scale quantitative research to understand how people interact with each other and the world around them. The findings are used to improve Facebook's product and identify new opportunities to help bring the world closer together. Various methods are used, including machine learning, field experiments, surveys, and visualizations.

Spotify

Spotify is an internationl digital music service that gives you access to millions of songs, podcasts, and videos from artists all over the world. Data science plays an integral part in understanding what songs or artists you like, what new genres of songs to recommend to you at any given moment in time, or deciding which new features to implement to increase user engagement.

Kaggle

Kaggle is part of Google and is an online community for data scientists. Users can find and publish data sets, explore and build models, work with other data scientists, and enter data science competitions to solve various problems. Companies routinely hold competitions and they usually attract hundreds or thousands of teams and individuals. In addition, Kaggle allow you to share Kaggle Kernels, which are notebooks that allow you to share code and analysis (in Python or R) with others. Kaggle Learn is its education offering, covering topics from Python and SQL to machine learning.

DeepMind
DeepMind is a an UK artificial intelligence company that was acquired by Google after demonstrating that the algorithms they built could surpass human level in various Atari video games. It also developed AlphaGo that ultimately led to the defeat of Lee Seedol, the world champion of the game Go.

Its ultimate goal is to solve intelligence by creating general-purpose learning algorithms capable of solving any task, just like the human brain can. DeepMind is currently working on a variety of AI topics, ranging from protein structure prediction and healthcare applications to AI ethics.

▶ **Consulting**
McKinsey & Company
McKinsey is a worldwide management consulting firm. In 2014, the firm opened McKinsey Solutions, a data, technology and analytics unit that employs data scientists, software/data engineers, and digital marketers. Data science can range from preparing data analysis to building models to help solve client problems in various industries. They operate in most industries, ranging from financial services and technology to energy and operations.

Boston Consulting Group (BCG)
BCG is another global management consulting firm. It also has a data science arm called BCG Gamma that helps organizations grow through applying data science and advanced technologies. They help build end-to-end solutions and tools for their clients.

Bain & Company
Bain is another global management consulting firm. Its data science arms are called Bain Vector and Bain Advanced Analytics. Data science consultants help extract value from data by developing and deploying advanced analytics to help turn data into a competitive advantage.

▶ **Travel and Transportation**
Uber
Uber is a ride-hailing company that connects drivers and riders. It doesn't own their own vehicles and relies on drivers (independent contractors). In addition, it offers food delivery and a system of electric bikes and scooters. Some applications of data science include:
- **Forecasting**: predicting supply and demand, real-time outages, hardware

capacity usage, fares, trip lengths, and traffic patterns

- **Risk:** identifying fraud and marketplace abuse, improving account security, minimizing credit risk for financial products, and detecting fake ratings and rides
- **Platforms:** developing platforms for forecasting, anomaly detection, computer vision, natural language processing, sensing and perception
- **Marketing:** develoing models to inform global marketing efforts

Airbnb

Airbnb is an online marketplace that lets people rent out their properties or spare rooms to guests. Similar to Uber, Airbnb does not own their own properties and rely on homeowners. Data scientists help improve the product by using data to improve search, provide better recommendations, determine host preferences, and predict future prices.

▶ Sports

NBA

The NBA (National Basketball Association) (as well as basketball teams) has access to lots of sports data, ranging from individual player statistics to game statistics. Basketball teams utilize data in an effort to build championship teams and help gain a winning advantage by analyzing other teams' strengths and weaknesses. Data is also used to understand which potential trades will be good (or bad) for a particular team.

▶ Politics

FiveThirtyEight

FiveThirtyEight is a website started by Nate Silver that focuses on opinion poll analysis, politics, economics, and sports. It originally started out as a model to predict how the 2008 elections would play out, ranging from the primary elections to the general election. The forecasting system he developed successfully predicted the outcome in 49 out of the 50 states in the 2008 US Presidential election and the outcome of all 50 states during the 2012 US Presidential election.

Cambridge Analytica Scandal

Cambridge Analytica was a political consulting firm that conducted work for the Trump campaign and collected data from around 87 million Facebook profiles, including information on public profiles, page likes, birthdays, and current cities. Other types of data included friends, News Feed posts, timelines, and messages. Once the data was collected, psychological profiles were created for each person, which helped indicate what kind of advertisements would be the most effective to persuade an individual to vote for a political event (namely, the election). This is an example of data science can be used in a nefarious manner.

XIII
Additional Questions

List of additional questions to help you prepare. Complete solutions are not written out yet but will be included in future editions and updates.

13.1 Suppose you are given the following datasets (all available in Kaggle), how would you go about analyzing:

1. **Lending Club Loan Data**: loan data for all loans issued between 2007-2015, including the current loan status (Current, Late, Fully Paid, etc.) and latest payment information. How would you predict who to loan to?

2. **2019 FIFA Game Results and FIFA 19 Complete Player Dataset**: how would you predict next year's results? How would you evaluate the offensive and defensive capabilities of every player?

3. **Heart Disease UCI**: contains 76 attributes and the "goal" field refers to the presence of heart disease in the patient (integer valued from 0 (no presence) to 4). How would you go about predicting who has heart disease?

Also feel free to actually analyze the data and share a Kaggle Kernel!

13.2 Given a user's chat history on Facebook Messenger (Instagram, Gmail, or Snapchat), how would you predict who he or she will send a message to?

13.3 Suppose you are Amazon. How would you go about deciding where to optimally place Amazon Lockers? What about Whole Foods?

13.3 Suppose you are given the task of optimizing a city's transportation system. How would you go about doing that? What metrics would you look at to determine success?

13.4 Suppose you are creating your own blockchain. How would go about testing how changing the transaction fees and block mining rates (or the difficulty of the cryptographic puzzle) affect the delays that the blockchain will encounter? (*hint*: use simulation)

13.5 Code up a solution to the knapsack problem using dynamic programming.

13.6 Create a graph of a network you find interesting: your friends, world leaders, flights, etc..

13.7 Find 5 data science related questions on Quora and answer them to the best of your knowledge.

13.8 How would you go about building a customized news feed to show the most relevant content for every user?

13.9 How would you go about building a dating site or app? What kind of algorithms would you use?

13.10 What are some examples of where data science has gone wrong and ended up with the wrong conclusions?

13.11 How would you go about detecting plagiarism?

13.12 Explain what confidence intervals are. How do you interpret them?

13.13 A farmer has 10 acres to plant wheat or rye and he has to plant at least 7 acres. However, he has only $1200 to spend and each acre of wheat costs $200 to plant and each acre of rye costs $100. In addition, the farmer has to finish planting in 12 hours and it takes an hour to plant an acre of wheat and 2 hours to plant an acre of rye. If the profit is $500 per acre of wheat and $300 per acre of rye, how many acres of each should be planted to maximize profits? (*hint*: use linear programming)

13.14 How would you go about augmenting a dataset of images for a computer vision problem?

I
Solutions to What is Data Science?

1.1 Google CRISP-DM. What is it and what are the steps?

Solution: CRISP-DM stands for cross-industry process for data mining and is a structured approach to planning a data mining project. It defines the typical phases of a project, the tasks involved, and the relationships between the tasks. The model consists of six phases:

- **Business Understanding**: understand the project objectives and requirements from a business standpoint and then converting it into a data mining problem
- **Data Understanding**: become familiar with the data; explore the initial data, identify the data quality, and discover initial insights (exploratory data analysis)
- **Data Preparation**: prepare the final dataset from the raw datasets (cleaning, imputation, merging, etc)
- **Modeling**: model the data using selected modeling techniques; if necessary, loop back to the previous step to prepare more data.
- **Evaluation**: compare the various models based on some evaluation metric and check that the models will generalize well; select the best model
- **Deployment**: deploying the model to work on new unseen data

1.2 Can you walk me through the steps in a data science project?

Solution: CRISP-DM is a valid answer. But could break it down even more:
1. Specify the objective.
2. Acquire the data.
3. Explore the data.
4. Establish a baseline.
5. Model the data.
6. Analyze the results.
7. Communicate findings.
8. Deploy and iterate.

1.3 Come up with 5 metrics of success for a:
- Video game with in-game purchases (Fortnite, Minecraft)
- Social networking product (Instagram, Snapchat)
- Advertisement-driven firm (YouTube, Google)
- Subscription based company (Netflix, Spotify)
- Ride-sharing company (Uber, Lyft)

Solution:

- Video Game
  1. **Daily Active Users:** number of daily users
  2. **Daily Session Duration:** average time a user is playing daily
  3. **Average Revenue:** average dollar amount a user is spending
  4. **Retention Rate:** how many users keep coming back to play
  5. **k-factor:** the viral growth rate of users converting non-users into users (number of invites by users x conversion rate per invite)
- Social Networking Product
  1. **User Growth:** how much the user base is growing
  2. **User Interaction:** number of daily posts or likes or shares
  3. **Average Engagement:** how long the average user using the product
  4. **Sales Revenue:** how much money the product is making
  5. **Web Traffic:** daily website visits
- Advertisement Driven
  1. **Return on Ad Spend (ROAS)**
  2. **Conversion Rate:** how often an ad click/view results in a purchase
  3. **Click-Through Rate:** number of times ad was clicked divided by the number of times it was shown
  4. **Earnings Per Click:** multiply conversion rate by average customer value
  5. **Time Watched:** if video ads, how long the ads were watched for
- Subscription Company
  1. **Annual Recurring Revenue:** revenue from repeat customers
  2. **Customer Lifetime Value:** monetary value of a customer's entire relationship with the company (present value of projected cash flows)
  3. **Customer Acquisition Cost:** cost of convincing a potential customer to subscribe
  4. **Churn Rates:** proportion of subscribers who leave during a time period; possible indicator of customer dissatisfaction
  5. **Average Revenue Per Account:** how much money you are making per customer
- Ride-Sharing Company
  1. **Supply and Demand:** how well does demand and supply match up (between drivers and riders)
  2. **Driver Ratings:** how highly rated the drivers are
  3. **New Rider Sign Ups:** how many new riders sign up per time period
  4. **Satisfactory Rides:** number of satisfactory rides divided by the total number of rides
  5. **Engagement Speed:** how fast is the demand from a rider met

---

1.4 What are some key business metrics for a:
- Bank
- Hedge Fund

- e-Commerce Site

Solution:
- Bank
  1. **Assets Under Management**: total monetary value of assets managed by the bank
  2. **Return on Equity:** total income divided by the total equity owned by shareholders
  3. **Return on Assets**: total income divided by total assets
  4. **New Accounts** Opened: number of new accounts opened in a time period
  5. **Expenses:** costs incurred during operations
- Hedge Fund
  1. **Sharpe Ratio**: average rate of return minus the risk-free rate divided by the standard deviation of return on the investments
  2. **Maximum Drawdown:** largest percentage decline of equity
  3. **Gain Pain Ratio**: ratio of the sum of the returns to the absolute value of the sum of all the negative returns
- Retail Bank
  1. **Shopping Cart Abandonment**: number of users who add products to the shopping cart but do not check out
  2. **Average Margin:** percentage that represents profit margin over a period of time
  3. **Cost of Goods Sold**: amount of money you are spending on manufacturing and selling the goods
  4. **Average Order Size**: how much a customer spends on a single order
  5. **Market Share**: how much your business comprises of the entire market compared to competitors

---

1.5 How do you test whether a new credit risk scoring model works? What data would you look at?

Solution: Assuming the credit risk scoring model was trained on a training set, continue to collect data similar to the training data and test the model on the new unseen data. If the test errors are similar to the training errors, then the model is working (also assuming that a model which was not working would never be deployed in the first place). The main idea is to test the model on an out-of-sample data set that comes from the same population as the training data.

1.6 What tools and packages do you work with and are comfortable with?

Solution: Whatever tools or packages that you use and are comfortable with using/talking about.

1.7 What is your favorite algorithm? Can you explain it to me in non-technical terms?

Solution: You must have a favorite algorithm by now. A tip to help formulate your answer is to use analogies and metaphors to help explain the concept.

1.8 Walk me through one of your data science projects. How did you approach it? What did you learn? What would you do differently now?

Solution: A tip while you are working through your data science projects is to jot down the assumptions you made, exactly what you did, and the thought process that led to it. Having everything jotted down somewhere will help you answer this question tremendously, as well help you clarify your thinking.

1.9 What are you learning about now? How do you keep up with the newest technologies?

Solution: Always be learning! The field is constantly evolving and changing, so always be learning and improving yourself. The best investment you can make is in yourself.

1.10 Which data scientists do you admire the most and why?

Solution: Pretty self-explanatory. Just a question to see how interested you really are in the field. If you've spent some time studying, you definitely would have stumbled across a few recurring names.

II
Solutions to Big Ideas in Data Science

2.1 Explain what regularization is and why it is useful.

Solution: Regularization is the process of adding a penalty to the cost function of a model to shrink the coefficient estimates. It is useful because it helps prevent overfitting. The most common forms are L1 (Lasso) and L2 (Ridge). One advantage of Lasso is that it can force coefficients to be zero and act as a feature selector.

2.2 How do you solve for multicollinearity?

Solution: Multicollinearity occurs when independent variables in a model are correlated. This is a problem mainly because it makes the model much more difficult to interpret. Suppose we have a linear regression model with correlated features X and Z as inputs and Y as the output. The true effect of X on Y is hard to differentiate from the true effect of Z on Y. Why? Because if we increase X, Z will also increase/decrease. The coefficient of X can be interpreted as the increase in Y for every unit we increase for X while *holding Z constant*. In addition, the standard errors become overinflated and makes some variables statistically insignificant when they should be significant.

To solve this issue, we can remove highly correlated features prior training the model (using forward or backward selection), use Lasso regularization to force coefficients to zero, or use PCA to reduce the number of features and end up with linear features.

2.3 What is overfitting and why is it a problem in machine learning models? What steps can you take to avoid it?

Solution: Overfitting occurs when a model fits too closely to the training data and just memorizes it. As a result, it generalizes poorly on future, unseen data. This is a problem because the model hasn't actually learned the signal (just the noise) and will have near-zero predictive capabilities.

Overfitting can be reduced by:
- Cross validation to estimate the model's performance on unseen data
- Ensembling techniques to reduce variance (bagging, stacking, blending)
- Regularization techniques that add a penalty to the cost function and makes models less flexible

2.4 Explain the difference between generative and discriminative algorithms.

Solution: Suppose we have a dataset with training input x and labels y. A generative model explicitly models the actual distribution of each class. It learns the joint probability distribution, p(x, y), and then uses Bayes' Theorem to calculate p(y|x). It then picks the most likely label y. Examples of generative classifiers include Naive Bayes, Bayesian Networks and Markov Random Fields.

A discriminative model directly learns the conditional probability distribution p(y|x) or a direct mapping from inputs x to the class labels y. This way, it models the decision boundary between the classes. Some popular discriminative classifiers include logistic regression, neural networks and nearest neighbors.

2.5 Explain the bias-variance tradeoff.

Solution: Bias is the error caused from oversimplification of your model (underfitting). Variance is the error caused from having a too complex model (overfitting). There exists a tradeoff because models with a low bias will usually have a higher variance and vice versa. The key is to minimize both bias and variance.

2.6 Is more data always better?

Solution: Not necessarily. This is related to the concept of Big Data Hubris or the idea that big data is a substitute, rather than a supplement to, traditional data collection and analysis. It also depends on the problem and the quality of data. If the data you keep collecting is constantly biased in some way, then obtaining more data is not helpful. Also keep in mind the tradeoff between having more data vs. dealing with additional storage, increased memory, and needing more computational power.

2.7 What are feature vectors?

Solution: A feature vector is a n-dimensional vector of numerical features that represent some object and can be represented as a point in n-dimensional space.

2.8 How do you know if one algorithm is better than others?

Solution: Better can mean a lot of different things: better on the training set? Several training sets? Faster? More space-efficient? It really depends on the problem, goal, and constraints.

2.9 Explain the difference between supervised and unsupervised machine learning.

Solution: In supervised machine learning algorithms, we have to provide labeled data (e.g. spam or not-spam, cats or not-cats) so the model can learn the mapping from inputs to labeled outputs. In unsupervised learning, we do not need to have labeled data and the goal is to detect patterns or learn representations of the data (e.g. detecting anomalies or finding similar groupings of customers.)

2.10 What is the difference between convex and non-convex functions?

Solution: A convex function has one minimum and this is important because an optimization algorithm (like gradient descent) won't get stuck in a local minimum. A non-convex function has some up-and-down valleys (local minimas) that aren't as down as the overall down (global minimum). Optimization algorithms can get stuck in the local minimum and it can be hard to tell when this happens.

2.11 Explain gradient descent. What is the difference between a local and global optimum?

Solution: Gradient descent is an optimization algorithm used to minimize some function by iteratively moving in the direction of steepest descent as defined by the negative of the gradient. By moving in the direction of the negative gradient, we slowly make our way down to a lower point until we get to the bottom (local minima). We use gradient descent to update the parameters of our model.

A local optimum is a solution that is the best solution among the neighboring solutions but is not the best solution overall. A global optimum is *the* best solution overall.

2.12 Suppose you have the following two lists: a = [42, 84, 3528, 1764] and b = [42, 42, 42, 42]. What does the following piece of code do? How can you make it run faster?

```
>>> total = 0
>>> for idx, val in enumerate(a):
>>>     total += a[idx] * b[idx]
>>> return total
```

Solution: Essentially the dot product between two 1-dimensional vectors. Can use np.dot(np.array(a), np.array(b)) instead.

III
Solutions to Mathematical Prerequisites

3.1 Define the Central Limit Theorem (CLT) and its importance.

Solution: The CLT states that if we repeatedly take independent random samples of size n from a population (for both normal and nonnormal data) and when n is large, the distribution of the sample means with approach a normal distribution. CLT allows us to make inferences from a sample about a population, without needing the characteristics of the whole population. Confidence intervals, hypothesis testing, and p-value analysis are all based on the CLT.

3.2 Define the Law of Large Numbers and its importance.

Solution: The LLN states that if an experiment is repeated independently a large number of times and you take the average of the results, the average should be close to the expected value (or the mathematically proven result). An example of this is tossing a coin 42x vs 42000000x; you will expect the percentage of heads/tails to be closer to 50% for the latter. This implies that large sample sizes are more reflective of reality than small sample sizes.

3.3 What is the normal distribution? What are some examples of data that follow it?

Solution: The normal distribution is a symmetric distribution where most of the observations cluster around the mean (68% of the values fall within one standard deviation of the mean, 95% fall within two standard deviations, and 99.7% fall within three). Height, weight, shoe size, test scores, blood pressure, and daily return of stocks are all examples.

3.4 How do you check if a distribution is close to normal?

Solution: One method to test for normality is to use Q-Q Plots. It is a graphical tool used to help asset if data came from a theoretical distribution (e.g. Normal or Exponential). A Q-Q plot is created by plotting two sets of quantiles against one another; if both sets of quantiles came from the same distribution, the points should form a line that is roughly straight. Another method is to use the Kolmogorov-Smirnov test.

3.5 What is a long-tailed distribution? What are some examples of data that follow it? Why is it important in machine learning?

Solution: A long-tailed distribution (or Pareto) is a distribution where the data is clustered around the head and gradually levels off to zero. In other words, a large number of occurrences is accounted for by a small number of items (also known as the 80-20 rule: roughly 80% of the effects come from 20% of the causes). Some examples include: frequency of earthquakes (large number of small magnitude earthquakes, few large magnitude ones) and search engines (few keywords that are commonly searched for). In machine learning, this can be applied by saying that only 20% of the data might be useful or that 80% of your time will be spent on one part of the data science project (usually data cleaning).

3.6 What is Ax=b? And how does one solve it?

Solution: Ax=b is one way to specify a set of linear equations. A is an (m, n) matrix, b is a vector with m entries, and x is an unknown vector with n entries (which we are trying to solve for). Ax means we are multiplying matrix A and vector x. Ax=b has a solution if and only if b is a linear combination of the columns of A.

- We can just find x by taking the inverse of A: $x = A^{-1}b$
- Or we can solve Ax=b by creating an augmented matrix [A b] by attaching b to A as a column on the right. We then reduce [A b] to reduced row echelon form. If you still have a system that is solvable, then any of its solutions will be a solution to your original equation.

3.7 How does one multiply matrices?

Solution: There are two types of matrix multiplication:
- Scalar Multiplication: every entry is multiplied by a number (scalar)
- Matrix Multiplication (Dot Product): multiply two matrices A and B together, but can only be done if the number of columns in matrix A equals the number of rows in matrix B. If the size of A is a x b and the size of B is b x c, the result is a matrix of size a x c. The multiplication is done by multiplying corresponding members from each matrix and then summing them up. Matrix multiplication is not commutative (AB != BA)

3.8 Explain what eigenvalues and eigenvectors are.

Solution: A scalar λ is called an eigenvalue of an n x n matrix A if there is a nontrivial solution x such that $Ax = \lambda x$ and x is the eigenvector corresponding to the eigenvalue λ.

3.9 Given two fair dice, what is the probability of getting scores that sum to 4 to 7?

Solution: When you roll 2 dice, there are possible 36 combinations.

- The number of totals that sum up to 4 are three (1,3), (2,2), (3,1). So $\frac{3}{36}$.
- The number of totals that sum up to 7 are 6: (1,6), (2,5), (3,4), (4,3), (5,2), (6,1). So $\frac{6}{36}$.

3.10 A jar has 1000 coins. 999 are fair and 1 is double-headed. You pick a coin at random and toss it 10 times and they all come up heads. What is the probability that the next toss is also a head?

Solution: This is a direct application of Bayes' theorem
- P(double-headed coin | 10 heads) = (P(10 heads | double-headed coin) P(double-headed coin)) / (P(10 heads | double-headed coin) P(double-headed coin) + P(10 heads | fair coin) P(fair coin))
- P(10 heads | double-headed coin) = 1
- P(double-headed coin) = 1/1000 = 0.001
- P(10 heads | fair coin) = $(\frac{1}{2})^{1}0$
- P(fair coin) = 999/1000 = 0.999
- P(double-headed coin | 10 heads) = (P(10 heads | double-headed coin) P(double-headed coin)) / (P(10 heads | double-headed coin) P(double-headed coin) + P(10 heads | fair coin) P(fair coin)) = (1 * 0.001) / (1 * 0.001 + 0.999 * 0.5^2) = 0.5062

3.11 You are offered a contract on a piece of land that is worth $800,000 50% of the time, $300,000 30% of the time and $100,000 20% of the time. The contract allows you to pay X dollars for a land appraisal and then you can decide whether or not to pay $200,000 for the land. How much is the contract worth? And what is X?

Solution: This is an expected value question.
- 50% of the time you will make $600,000 ($800,000 - $200,000)
- 30% of the time you will make $1000,000 ($300,000 - $200,000)
- 20% of the time you will lose $1000,000 ($100,000 - $200,000)

The value of the contract without an appraisal is: 50% * 600,000 + 30% * 100,000 - 20% * 100,000 = 310,000

If you do pay X to determine the land's value, you don't buy the land if it's worth less than $200,000 (so 20% of the time you don't buy). Thus, the average profit will be 50% * 600,000 + 30% * 100,000 = 330,000. So, in other words, you will not be willing to pay more than $20,000 for an appraisal (330,000 - 310,000).

3.12 Suppose a life insurance company sells a $240,000 policy with a one year term to a 24 year old woman for $240. The estimated probability that she survives the year is .999562. What is the expected value of this policy for the insurance company?

Solution:
P(company gains money) = 0.999562
Amount of money the company gains = $240

P(company loses money) = 0.000438
Amount of money the company loses (if woman dies) = $240,000 $240 = $239,760

Expected value of policy = ($240)(0.999562) - ($240,000)(0.000438) = $134.77488

3.13 Suppose a disease has a 42% death rate. What's the probability that exactly 4 out of 12 randomly selected patients survive?

Solution: We can use the binomial distribution: $P(X = x) = \binom{n}{k}p^x(1-p)^{n-x} = \binom{12}{4}(0.42)^4(1 - 0.42)^{12-4} = 0.19725$

3.14 A roulette wheel has 38 slots- 18 are red, 18 are black, and 2 are green. You play 42 games and always bet on red. What is the probability that you win all 42 games?

Solution: $(18/38)^{42}$

3.15 Walk me through the steps of how you would set up an A/B test.

Solution: A/B testing is just an experimental design. The high-level steps are:

- **Define the Objective:** choose one metric to focus on and state your hypothesis
- **Create the Control and Test:** the control is the feature or website that you want to test against. For example, the control might be the website you have right now and the test is another website that has something different and you want to see if that difference is significant.
- **Collect the Data:** split your sample size equally and randomly then record the outcomes; usually the number of users participating in the A/B test is a small portion of the total users; the sample size you decide on will determine how long you will have to wait until you have collected enough data
- **Analyze the Results::** accept or reject the null hypothesis and determine if the results were significant enough

IV
Solutions to Computer Science Prerequisites

4.1 Compare R and Python.

Solution:
- R
  - Focuses on better, user friendly data analysis, statistics and graphical models
  - Large number of packages
  - Mainly used when analysis is performed on a single server
- Python
  - Interpreted and object-oriented language
  - General purpose
  - Huge ecosystem and community support
  - Simple and easy to understand

Honestly both are great choices and it comes down to a personal preference. You will get the same amount of work done using either language.

4.2 What libraries for data analysis do you know in Python/R?

Solution:
- R: dplyr, plyr, ggplot2, caret, etc.
- Python: pandas, NumPy, SciPy, scikit-learn, matplotlib, etc.

4.3 What are constraints in SQL?

Solution: Constraints are used to specify the rules concerning data in the table and can be applied for single or multiple fields in a table. Constraints include:
- NOT NULL: restricts NULL value from being inserted into a column
- CHECK: verifies that all values in a field satisfy a condition
- DEFAULT: automatically assigns a default value if no value has been specified for the field
- UNIQUE: ensures unique values to be inserted into the field
- INDEX: indexes a field providing faster retrieval of records
- PRIMARY KEY: uniquely identifies each record in a table
- FOREIGN KEY: ensures referential integrity for a record in another table

4.4 What is a primary key?

Solution: The primary key uniquely identifies each row in a table and must be unique values and not null. A table is restricted to have only one primary key, which is comprised of single or multiple fields.

4.5 What is a foreign key?

Solution: A foreign key comprises of single or collection of fields in a table that refers to the primary key in another table and used to link two tables together. The table containing the foreign key is called the child table and the table containing the candidate key is called the parent table (or referenced table).

4.6 What is a join? List its different types?

Solution: A join is used to combine records (rows) from two or more tables in a SQL database based on a related column between the tables. There are four types of joins:

- **Inner**: retrieves records that have matching values in both tables involved in the join
- **Left Outer Join**: retrieves all the records from the left table and the matched records from the right table
- **Right Outer Join**: retrieves all the records from the right table and the matched records from the left table
- **Full Outer Join**: retrieves all the records where there is a match in either the left or right table

4.7 What is a self-join?

Solution: Special case of a regular join where a table is joined to itself based on some relation between its own column(s) and uses an inner join or left join and a table alias (to assign different names to the table within the query)

4.8 What is a query? What is a subquery?

Solution: A query is a request for data or information from a database table or multiple tables; a subquery is a query within another query (nested query) and is used to return data to the main query as a condition to restrict the data to be retrieved.

4.9 Write a SQL query to get the third highest salary of an employee from table EMPLOYEES with two columns: name and salary.

Solution: Can use a subquery to first get the top 3, then order by salary ascending and select the top 1

SELECT TOP 1 salary FROM(
    SELECT TOP 3 salary
    FROM EMPLOYEES

ORDER BY salary DESC) AS employee
ORDER BY salary ASC;

4.10 Let's say you have two SQL tables: ARTISTS and SONGS. The ARTISTS table has columns artist_name and song_name. The SONGS table has columns song_name and sold_copies. Write a SQL query that shows the TOP 3 artists who sold the most songs in total.

Solution:
SELECT ARTISTS.artist_name, SUM(SONGS.sold_copies) AS sold_sum
FROM ARTISTS
JOIN SONGS
ON SONGS.song_name = ARTISTS.song_name
GROUP BY ARTISTS.artist_name
ORDER BY sold_sum DESC
LIMIT 3;

4.11 You have two SQL tables EMPLOYEES and SALARIES. EMPLOYEES has columns employee_name, employee_id, and department_name. SALARIES has columns employee_name, employee_id, and employee_salary. Write a SQL that displays all the departments where the average salary is less than $420.

Solution:
SELECT department_name, AVG(SALARIES.salary) AS avg_salaries
FROM EMPLOYEES
JOIN SALARIES
ON EMPLOYEES.employee_id = SALARIES.employee_id
GROUP BY department_name
HAVING AVG(SALARIES.salary) < 420;

4.12 Explain the star schema.

Solution: Traditional database schema with a central fact table (record measurements or metrics for a specific event such as sales) and satellite dimension tables map (reference data about the fact such as date). These dimension tables can be joined to the central fact table using the ID fields and are particularly useful in real-time applications, as they save a lot of memory. It's called a star schema because each fact is surrounded by its associated dimensions and resembles a star.

4.13 Explain the snowflake schema.

Solution: Database schema with a central fact table (record measurements or metrics for a specific event such as sales) and satellite dimension tables map (reference data about the fact such as date). However, in this case, the dimension tables can be further divided into additional tables. This results in potentially many joins to query the data (compared to a sinlge join fro the star schema).

4.14 What is the difference between SQL and NoSQL databases? What are some examples of each?

Solution: NoSQL databases have more flexible schemas, while SQL databases have a tabular relationship
- **Key-value**: in a key-value NoSQL database, all of the data within consists of an indexed key and a value (e.g. Cassandra, DynamoDB)
- **Document Database**: map a key to some document that contains structured information. The key is used to retrieve the document (e.g. MongoDB, CouchDB)
- **Graph Database**: designed for data whose relations are well-represented as a graph and has elements which are interconnected, with an undetermined number of relations between them (e.g. Polyglot Neo4J)

4.15 What is MapReduce? How would you use MapReduce to count words in a text corpus?

Solution: MapReduce is a framework for processing large datasets in a distributed fashion using several machines. The main idea is mapping your dataset into a collection of <key, value> pairs and then reducing over all pairs using the same keys.
- **Splitting**: the input is split across different machines
- **Mapping**: each machine takes its input and maps it to ¡key, value¿ pairs according to your logic. For example, for word count frequency the ¡key, value¿ would be: <word, 1>. This part does not aggregation, which is done in the reduce script.
- **Shuffling**: emitted <key, value> pairs are then shuffled or that pairs with the same key are moved to the same machine, which then runs the reduce script
- **Reducing**: takes in a collection of <key, value> pairs and reduces them. For example, for word count, we would take the sum of the collection of <key, value> pairs that share the same key.

V
Solutions to Exploratory Data Analysis

5.1 Explain why data cleaning is so important.

Solution: Dirty data will lead models to incorrect conclusions and insights, which might, in turn, drive an organization down the wrong path and strategy.

5.2 What is exploratory data analysis and why is it important?

Solution: EDA is the process that uses visual and statistical methods to understand and summarize a dataset without making any assumptions. It provides the knowledge necessary to develop the appropriate model and correctly interpret the results. It allows data scientists to be certain that the results are valid and applicable to the business problem. Skipping EDA can cause data scientists to generate inaccurate models, generate accurate models on the wrong data, incorrectly create the right types of variables during feature engineering, and generally waste time and resources.

5.3 How would you go about to produce high quality data?

Solution: The process would be to:
- Inspect the data for dirty data, compile summary statistics, and visualize the data
- Clean the data by dropping duplicates or irrelevant data, scale and impute the data, etc.
- Verify that the data is still valid
- Generate a data quality report that documents what changes were made

5.4 How do you inspect and deal with missing data?

Solution: You can use Python to count the number of NaNs. To deal with missing data, you can:
- Just drop the record with missing values
- Impute using the mean, median, mode
- Use linear regression to predict the missing values

5.6 What is the standard deviation of the following: [4, 2, 7, 12, 17, 6]?

Solution:
- Mean $= \frac{(4+2+7+12+17+6)}{6} = 8$
- Subtract the mean from each value and square the result:

$$- (4 - 8)^2 = 16$$
$$- (2 - 8)^2 = 36$$
$$- (7 - 8)^2 = 1$$
$$- (12 - 8)^2 = 16$$
$$- (17 - 8)^2 = 81$$
$$- (6 - 8)^2 = 4$$

- Mean of squared differences: $\frac{(16+36+1+16+81+4)}{6} = 25.67$ (divide by $N - 1$ if sample and not population)
- Then take the square root: $\sqrt{25.67} = 5.07$

5.7 Suppose you work for a cloud storage company and you analyze the amount of content uploaded every month. During early November, you notice a spike in picture uploads. What could be the cause of the spike and how would you test for it?

Solution: It's hard to say for certain what caused the spike, since causal relationships cannot be established with observed data. But we can perform a t-test (tests for significant differences between the means of two groups) by comparing the number of uploads in early November to the number of uploads for all of the other months.

VI
Solutions to Feature Engineering

6.1 Which is better: good data or good models? And how do you define good?

Solution: Good data is certainly more important than good models. Good data means that the data is clean and relevant to the problem at hand. Good models mean that the models generalize well to new and unseen data, as well as being relevant to the problem at hand.

6.2 Is there a universal good model? Are there any models that are definitely not so good?

Solution: The No Free Lunch Theorem states that there is no single algorithm that will work for every problem and that no single algorithm will be the best for all problems. In other words, there is no universal good model. By the same logic, certain models are useful in certain scenarios, so no model is definitely not so good. *"All models are wrong but some are useful"* -George E.P. Box

6.3 How to deal with unbalanced data classes (for classification)?

Solution: Unbalanced data can be dealt in multiple ways as listed below (considering more data cannot be collected):
- **Under-sampling**: eliminates majority class examples until data is balanced
- **Over-sampling**: increases number of instances in minority class by adding copies of those instances. This can be done randomly or synthetically using Synthetic Minority (SMOTE).
- **Use suitable evaluation metrics**: accuracy can be a misleading metric for unbalanced data. Suitable metrics would include Precision, Recall, F1-score, AUC, etc.
- **Sample Weights**: provide higher weights for the samples in the minority class so the classifier puts more emphasis on getting these samples right

6.4 Suppose we are building a fraud detection system and have all the transaction data for the past week for users (date, location, and amount). What kind of new features can we engineer?

Solution: Be creative! Below are some examples:
- Number of transactions in the past x hours
- Rate of increased transactions in the past x hours
- Total amount of transactions in the past x hours

- Number of transactions at different locations
- If we have the user's home address, create an indicator variable (1 or 0) denoting if transaction took place near home
- Distance from user's home to location of transaction

6.5 What is TF-IDF?

Solution: TF-IDF stands for term frequency-inverse document frequency and is a numerical statistic that represents how important a word is to a document in a collection. The value increases with respect to the number of times a word appears in a document, but is offset by the number of documents that contain the word. So words that are common in every document (the, this, if) rank lower even though they appear many times because they don't mean much to that document. For example, if "Meeseek" appears many times in a document but not in others, it implies that it is important to that document.

6.6 What are feature interactions?

Solution: When features interact with each other and cannot be expressed as the sum of the feature effects because the value of one feature depends on the value of the other feature.

6.7 What is an n-gram? What are some possible use cases?

Solution: An n-gram is simply a sequence of n words. We can assign probabilities to the occurrence of an n-gram or the probability of a word occurring next in a sequence of words. Then we can make predictions about which n-grams belong together, make predictions about the next word, and even make corrections in spelling. The n-gram model is widely used in NLP.

6.8 What is the 2-gram for the following phrase: "The answer to the ultimate question of life, the universe and everything is 42." What about the 3-gram?

Solution: Assuming we ignore punctuation and spaces:
- 2-gram: "The answer", "answer to", "to the", "the ultimate", "ultimate question", "question of", "of life", "life the", "the universe", "universe and", "and everything", "everything is", "is 42"
- 3-gram: "The answer to", "answer to the", "to the ultimate", "the ultimate question", "ultimate question of", "question of life", "of life the", "life the universe", "the universe and", "universe and everything", "and everything is", "everything is 42"

VII
Solutions to Evaluation Metrics

7.1 Suppose you have trained many different models. How do you select the best one?

Solution: One of the most common ways is to use cross-validation to test the how well a model will generalize to new and unseen data (not the training data). The model with the best validation results can be considered the "best" model.

However, this is only the best model with respect to validation scores. Other best models could be respect to computation cost, space efficiency, interpretability, etc. So "best" really depends on the problem.

7.2 Suppose you have one model and you want to find the best set of parameters. How do you go about doing that?

Solution: Hyperparameter tuning. We can train the model several times with various hyperparameters and then keep track of the results of each iteration. When the model has tested out all of the possible hyperparameters, you can select the best model based on an evaluation metric.

The steps in hyperparameter tuning are:
1. Define a model
2. Define the range of possible values for all hyperparameters
3. Define a method for sampling hyperparameter values
   - **Exhaustive Grid Search**: simply build a model for each possible combination all of the hyperparameter values
   - **Random Search**: search over random combinations of all the hyperparameter values by sampling each hyperparameter value from a distribution. This is advantageous over exhaustive search since the run time is much lower but may result in slightly worse performance due to higher variance.
4. Define an evaluation metric to judge the model
5. Define a cross-validation technique

7.3 Explain what precision and recall are. How do they relate to the ROC curve?

Solution: Precision is how often the classifier is correct when it predicts positive and recall is the ratio of correct predictions over total predictions. The ROC curve shows how the recall and precision relationship changes as the thresholds for identifying a positive changes in the model by plotting the true positive rate (TPR) and the false positive rate (FPR) as a function of a model's threshold.

7.4 Is it better to have too many false positives, or too many false negatives? Explain.

Solution: It depends on the problem but let us examine a few examples:
- For HIV testing, a false negative occurs when the test identifies that the disease is absent when it is actually present. This may result in inadequate treatment of the disease and increase the risk of the patient spreading the virus to others. So, in this scenario, having more false positives is preferable to having more false negatives.
- For spam filtering, a false positive occurs when a spam filter wrongly identifies a legitimate email as spam and the email is not received. In this case, the receiver might rather prefer some spam emails in their inbox than have an important email go to spam. So, in this scenario, having more false negatives is preferable to having more false positives.

7.5 What is cross-validation? How do you do it right?

Solution: Cross-validation is a technique for evaluating how well a model will generalize to a previously unseen data set and more importantly, how well it will perform in practice. However, the way the testing and validation data sets are drawn depends on the problem and they should be drawn from the same population. For example, for time series data, it doesn't make sense to randomly assign points to training and testing data. A few methods to conduct cross validation are leave-one-out cross-validation (LOOCV) and k-fold.

7.6 Is it better to design robust or accurate algorithms?

Solution: It depends on the problem but the goal of any algorithm is for it to be robust and generalize well on previously unseen data. Again there is a trade-off between bias and variance; having more complex models will lead to higher accuracy but may not be robust and vice versa.

7.7 How do you define/select evaluation metrics?

Solution: The type of evaluation metric depends on a few factors:
- Regression or classification?
- Business objective?
- What metric should we optimize for?
- What is the distribution of the target variable?

VIII
Solutions to Supervised Learning

8.1 Describe the regression problem. What is the goal?

Solution: The regression problem is the task of approximating a function f(x) from input features X to a continuous output Y. This is different than classification where the output Y is a discrete set of class labels.

8.2 Explain linear regression.

Solution: Linear regression is a model that assumes the data is linear and fits a line through the data so that the distance between the points and the line is minimized. The line is of the form $Y = \beta_0 + \beta_1 X_1 + ... + \beta_p X_p + \epsilon$ and the goal is to find the optimal coefficients $B_0...B_p$. Future predictions are made by inputting a new feature vector X into trained regression equation.

8.3 What is the OLS Regression formula? How do you solve for it?

Solution: OLS stands for Ordinary Least Squares and is a method to estimate the unknown parameters/coefficients in the linear regression model. OLS is based on the principle of least squares or minimizing the sum of squares differences between the true values of Y and the predicted values $\hat{Y}$ (from our model). To solve for OLS, we can use:

- Gradient descent to find the parameters that minimize the cost function.
- Matrix form (linear algebra) and solve for the parameters in closed-form since linear regression is just a set of linear equations and can be formulated as Ax=b (or $Xw = y$), where w is the coefficent vector . Thus rearranging the formula gives us: $w = (X^T X)^{-1} X^T y$. The downside of solving it in closed-form is that inverting X might be very expensive (maybe even impossible) if X becomes too large.

8.4 Is the intercept term necessary? Why do we need it?

Solution: The intercept term in linear regression represents the mean of the response Y when all the predictors or features are all 0; $X_i = 0 \ \forall i$. It also forces the residuals to have mean zero and makes sure that the coefficient estimates are unbiased.

8.5 Compare OLS to Lasso and Ridge.

Solution: OLS stands for Ordinary Least Squares where the loss function is the sum of squares differences. Ridge and Lasso are two regularization techniques

104

that modify the loss function by penalizing the size of the coefficients in order to shrink them towards zero.

- **Lasso Regression**: adds the absolute value of the magnitude of the coefficients as the penalty term to the loss function. This can cause some coefficients to shrink exactly to zero, which functions as a feature selector.
- **Ridge Regression**: adds the squared value of the magnitude of the coefficients as the penalty term but doesn't force coefficients to zero and will result in a model with all the features.

8.6 What are the assumptions for linear regression? What if some are violated?

Solution: The assumptions are:

- Representative: the training data used to fit the model is representative of the population
- Linearity: relationship between X and Y is linear
- Homoscedasticity: variance of residuals is the same for any value of X
- Independence: errors are uncorrelated
- Normality: error distribution is normal

The normality assumptions of linear regression actually doesn't apply to X and Y, only to the errors. In addition, the assumptions are usually violated in real life but if the training data is large enough and the deviation from normality is not too great, then the results should be fairly close to what you would get if the assumptions were not violated.

8.7 How do you interpret the coefficients? How do you determine the significant features?

Solution: The sign of a regression coefficient tells you if there exists a positive or negative correlation between each independent variable and the dependent variable. A positive (negative) coefficient tells us that as the value of the independent variable increases (decreases), the dependent variable also increases (decreases).

The value of the coefficient also tells us how significant the coefficient is- the value represents how much the dependent variable changes given a one-unit change in the independent variable while holding other variables in the model constant. Holding the other variables constant is crucial because it allows you to assess the effect of each variable in isolation from the others (something that you cannot do accurately if multicollinearity exists between the variables).

8.8 Do you think 50 small decision trees are better than a large one? Why? How would you combine small trees?

Solution: Yes (usually). Having 50 of the same decision trees is not very helpful and having one large decision tree (grown to the full depth) would probably overfit the data. But if the 50 trees were trained as a random forest, where each tree is trained on a different subset of the training data and only considering a subset of the features, this would help reduce variance and be less prone to overfitting. In addition, if the trees were boosted by training each tree sequentially and each tree focused on what the previous trees missed, then the 50 trees would most certainly be better.

8.9 What is the maximal margin classifier?

Solution: The maximal margin classifier is the SVM classifier. The goal is to find the best hyperplane, or the one that maximizes the distance to the closest data points from both classes. However, this assumes that the data is linearly separable since such a hyperplane would never exist if the data was not. The soft margin classifier allows points to be on the wrong side of the hyperplane.

8.10 What is deep learning?

Solution: Deep learning is a subfield of machine learning that is loosely based on the structure of the human brain. It is comprised on neurons (nonlinear activation functions) that are interconnected (by weights). The weights are trained and tuned so that certain neurons are activated when presented with a certain input. A collection of neurons and weights is called a neural network and they are also universal approximators, meaning there exists a neural network that can approximate any function.

8.11 How would you build a model to predict credit card fraud?

Solution: There are potentially two approaches:
- **Classic Approach**: build an expert-based system. In other words, build a system based on the experience and domain knowledge of a fraud analyst. This typically involves a manual investigation of a suspicious case and may indicate that a new method to commit fraud has been developed. The solution to catch the fraud method or pattern is often implemented as a rule (If-Then rules that capture the newly detected fraud methods). These rules are then used collectively to capture future transactions or cases.
- **Automated Approach**: build an automated fraud-detection system that requires less human involvement and could lead to more efficient and effective systems for fraud detection. First collect the relevant data, then develop the model, and last monitor/update the model. However, this would still require domain knowledge and input of a fraud analyst to engineer the necessary features. Such an approach can be more precise and more operationally/cost efficient.

IX

Solutions to Unsupervised Learning

9.1 What is the purpose of dimensionality reduction? What is it used for? What methods do you know?

Solution: The goal of dimensionality reduction is to reduce the dimensions of your feature set by either removing some or combining them. You might want to consider dimensionality reduction when you have too many features to consider, have correlated features, or just have useless features. Some methods include PCA, LDA, feature selection (Forward, Backward) and t-SNE.

9.2 What is the cluster analysis problem? What clustering methods do you know?

Solution: The cluster analysis problem of grouping similar data points into groups or clusters. Similarity is tricky and must be defined properly to ideally find the similarities we are looking for. Some clustering algorithms are k-means clustering and hierarchical clustering.

9.3 How do you take millions of Apple users (with hundreds of transactions each and among thousands of products) and group them into meaningful segments?

Solution: There are two approaches:
1. **Manual Approach**: we can segment the market based on domain knowledge. For example, we can group Apple's products into four main lines:
   - Mac: within this line we have the education segment which consists of teachers, students, and schools. Schools will usually pair with Apple to offer discounted products, which affect teacher and student purchases. So targeting schools with Apple products might help boost sales for both teachers and students. Teachers will also buy Macs to educate the students, which further influence the students to do the same. So targeting teachers may help boost sales for students. We can obviously continue to segment the Mac line into other segments such as leisure, corporate, etc...
   - iPhone: perhaps in this line we can segment users into tech savvy and not-so tech savvy. Tech savvy meaning they are always up to date with the latest technologies and not-so meaning they are ok with buying the latest model a few months or years later.
   - iPad: maybe we can segment this line into leisure (brings entertainment through games or books) and business (lightweight and lets users get work done).
   - iPod: it is possible that most adults would rather buy an iPhone instead of an iPod, so maybe the biggest segment could be kids whose

parents don't want them to have a phone yet.

2. Clustering Approach

- We can group similar users using user information (gender, spending, recent purchases, purchase items) to discover user segments. An example of a cluster we find is a high spender cluster that has high spending in the past 12 months and frequent purchases. Once a cluster is determined, a marketing strategy can be formulated accordingly.

9.4 Explain what a local optimum is and why it is important in a specific context, such as k-means clustering. What are specific ways of determining if you have a local optimum problem? What can be done to avoid them?

Solution: A local minima is a solution that is the best solution for the points around it. In other words, it's not the best solution overall but it may be a pretty good solution. In k-means, it means we have found a set of clusters but it might not be the best set of clusters. We can try:

- To run the algorithm with different centroid initializations
- Adjust the number of iterations
- Actually find out the optimal number of clusters

9.5 Is feature scaling important prior to applying k-means clustering? If so, why?

Solution: Yes. Feature scaling ensures that all the features have the same weight during the clustering analysis. Consider a scenario of clustering people based on their weights (in kilos) with a range of 55-110 and height (in inches) with range 5.0-6.4. In this case, the clusters produced without scaling can be very misleading since weight will dominate the height feature.

9.6 What is a method for finding an optimal number of cluster in k-means? How do you determine the quality of a clustering?

Solution: The elbow method is a heuristic used for finding the optimal number of clusters by looking at the percentage of variance explained as a function of the number of clusters. A good number of clusters is when adding another cluster does not give result in a significant increase in variance explained.

We can also look at the MSE to determine how good a clustering is.

9.7 What should be the best choice for number of clusters using the elbow method based on the following k-means results:

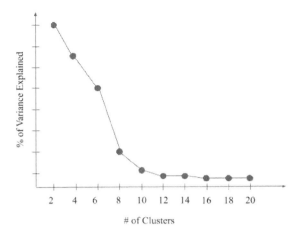

# of Clusters

Solution: Based on the above results, the best choice of number of clusters using elbow method is 10.

9.8 What are some stopping conditions for k-means?

Solution: A few include:
- Fixed number of iterations
- Assignment of observations to clusters stop changing
- Centroids stop changing
- MSE falls below a certain threshold

9.9 Assume you want to cluster 7 observations into 3 clusters using k-means. After the first iteration, clusters C1, C2, C3 have the following observations:
- C1: $(2, 1)$, $(3, 2)$, $(7, 3)$
- C2: $(2, 4)$, $(5, 2)$
- C3: $(3, 3)$, $(7, 7)$

What are the new cluster centroids?

Solution: The centroid calculation are as follows:
- Centroid $C_1 = (\frac{(2+3+7)}{3}, \frac{(1+2+3)}{3}) = (4, 2)$
- Centroid $C_2 = (\frac{(2+5)}{2}, \frac{(4+2)}{2}) = (3.5, 3)$
- Centroid $C_3 = (\frac{(3+7)}{2}, \frac{(3+7)}{2}) = (5, 5)$

9.10 Explain how you would go about building a recommender system.

Solution: A recommender system is an algorithm whose goal is to suggest relevant items to users, where items can be anything from what movies to watch, books or news to read or products to buy. Certain recommender systems can be crucial in certain industries to generate huge amounts of income such as Netflix, Amazon, and YouTube. One popular method is called collaborative filtering, which utilizes user interactions to filter for items of interest and is based on the assumption that if a user likes item A and another user likes item A too and another item B, then the first user could potentially be interested in item B as well.

- **Memory-Based**: the first approach is memory-based, which identifies clusters of users and utilizes the interactions of one specific user to predict the interactions of other similar users. Another way is to identify clusters of items that have been rated by user A and uses them to predict the interaction of user A with a different but similar item B. The downside with a memory-based approach is that we might run into sparse matrices, since the number of user-item interactions can be too low to generate high quality clusters.

- **Model-Based**: the second approach is model-based which trains models to make predictions. For example, one could use existing user-item interactions to train a model to predict the Top 5 items that a user might like the most.

9.11 How is k-NN different from k-means clustering?

Solution: k-NN (k-nearest neighbors) is a supervised learning algorithm, where the k is an integer describing the number of neighboring data points that vote on the final result. k-means is an unsupervised clustering algorithm, where the k is an integer describing the number of clusters to be created from the given data.

X
Solutions to Reinforcement Learning

10.1 What are some real-life potential use cases for reinforcement learning agents?

Solution: Some applications are:
- Resource management: allocate resources efficiently (such as power grids)
- Traffic light control: display optimal traffic lights at appropriate times to reduce congestion
- Robotics: learning to navigate various terrains (potentially extraterrestrial) and perform different tasks
- Games: learning to play and beat various games

10.2 Check out OpenAI and build a RL algorithm in Python for the game Cartpole.

Solution: Check out the Cracking the Data Science Interview Github page for guides and code.

References

Hastie, Trevor, et al. *The Elements of Statistical Learning, Second Edition: Data Mining, Inference, and Prediction.* Springer, 2009.

James, Gareth, et al. *An Introduction to Statistical Learning: with Applications in R.* Springer, 2017.

Molnar, Christoph. *Interpretable machine learning. A Guide for Making Black Box Models Explainable,* 2019. https://christophm.github.io/interpretable-ml-book/.

Skiena, Steven S. *Data Science Design Manual.* Springer, 2018.

Weinberger, Killian. *Machine Learning for Intelligent Systems.* Cornell University. Lecture Notes, 2018. https://www.cs.cornell.edu/courses/cs4780/2018fa/.

Printed in Great Britain
by Amazon